FAME

Based on the screenplay by **CHRISTOPHER GORE**.

Conceived by **DAVID DE SILVA**.

Adapted to the stage by **CHRISTOPHER SERGEL**.

THE DRAMATIC PUBLISHING COMPANY

FAME
A Full-Length Play
for Fifteen Women and Nine Men, Extras as desired

CHARACTERS

The Faculty

MRS. SHERWOOD . . . . teaches English

MISS BERG . . . . teaches dance

MR. FARRELL . . . . teaches acting

MR. SHOROFSKY . . . . teaches music

The Students

DORIS	SHIRLEY
COCO	LYDIA
PHENICIA	LEROY
MICHAEL	NICOLE
LISA	MARIANNE
DEIRDRE	HILARY
JOY	RALPH
BRUNO	MONTGOMERY

Relatives of the Students

MRS. SCHWARTZ . . . . the mother of Doris

ANGELO. . . . . Bruno's father

MARIO . . . . Bruno's uncle

and At the Cabaret

MISTRESS OF CEREMONIES

TIME: The Present

PLACE: The School of Performing Arts
West 46th Street, New York City

SPECIAL LYRICS FOR THE FINALE
WRITTEN BY
DAVID ROGERS.

ACT ONE

The houselights dim to black.

Then a pin spot comes up on the face of a sensitive, good looking young man at DC.

MONTGOMERY. I always worry that maybe people aren't going to like me when I go to a party. Isn't that crazy? Do you ever get kind of a sick feeling in the pit of your stomach when you dread things? Gee, I wouldn't want to miss a party for anything. But every time I go to one . . . I keep feeling that the whole world's against me. See, I've spent almost my whole life in military academies. My mother doesn't have a place for me where she lives. She . . . she just doesn't know what else to do with me. But you mustn't misunderstand about my mother. She's really a very lovely person . . . (There is more light and we can see that MONTGOMERY is standing in front of the curtains.) . . . I guess every boy thinks his mother is beautiful, but my mother really is. She tells me in every letter she writes how sorry she is that we can't be together more, but she has to think of her work. One time we were together, though. She met me in San Francisco once and we were together for two whole days. Just like we were sweethearts. It was the most wonderful time I ever had. And then I had to go back to the military academy. Every time I walk into the barracks . . . (He has difficulty with the lines.) . . . I get kind of a depressed feeling. It's got hard stone walls . . . You know what I mean. Well, gee! (He chokes.) I guess I've bored you enough, telling you about myself.

ADULE MALE VOICE (from the darkness at L). Thank you.

MONTGOMERY (holding up a playbook, nervously). The monologue is from *The Dark at the Top of the Stairs*.

ADULT MALE VOICE. I know. (Firmly.) Thank you.

MONTGOMERY (unhappily). I goofed the last couple lines. Nervous I guess. If you'd like, I could . . .

(The man who has been sitting in a folding chair at L, his back to the audience, is MR. FARRELL, head of the Drama Department. He gets up and approaches MONTGOMERY.)

MR. FARRELL. That's okay. (He glances at his clipboard.) Montgomery MacNeill. You did very well. (As MONTGOMERY starts to say something more, he stops him.) And — thank you.

MONTGOMERY (stopping, defeated, exiting). Yes. Sure.

(MRS. SHERWOOD, an English teacher, enters L and comes up to MR. FARRELL as MONTGOMERY exits R.)

MRS. SHERWOOD (nodding after MONTGOMERY). How was that one?

MR. FARRELL. He did the lines without trying to put in a lot of feeling. I like that. The loneliness . . . the abandonment . . . They're already in the lines.

MRS. SHERWOOD. And?

MR. FARRELL (making a check on the clipboard). He's . . . in.

MRS. SHERWOOD. How many that you've heard today are . . . out?

MR. FARRELL (showing the clipboard to MRS. SHERWOOD). Suppose one of these bad auditions was just extreme nerves — and the girl might have gone on to be another Jane Fonda or Colleen Dewhurst? Or the boy a young Sidney Poitier?

MRS. SHERWOOD. I'm glad I just teach English. I don't have to stand at the gate saying "no."

MR. FARRELL (waving the clipboard, with a big smile). I just had a yes. (He starts off L, calling as he goes.) Next.

MRS. SHERWOOD (looking front). Auditions for the School of Performing Arts, P.A. for short. The chance of being accepted is about one out of fifty-seven. Unless you're a boy applying to the Dance Department. They need boys. Or someone who can play violin. The Music Department needs strings.

(The curtain rises behind MRS. SHERWOOD to reveal a stage of several levels with areas that separately suggest a dance practice area, a music room, a part of a classroom, and an open central playing area. A few applicant STUDENTS are discovered onstage warming up bodies, vocal chords or rechecking audition scenes.)

MRS. SHERWOOD (continuing). This seedy wreck of a building was old when George Burns was a boy. Built in 1908 as a fire-house, it passed through a lot of hands, and when they ran out of sensible possibilities, someone allotted it to a high school with dance, music, and drama departments. (She considers the STUDENTS onstage.) The performing arts.

(More applicant STUDENTS enter and join those already onstage.

Some of them come down the aisles, talking to each other as they come. Most are dressed in jeans but some are in tights or tutus. They carry bags, shoes, playbooks and instruments.)

MRS. SHERWOOD (continuing over the noise). Eartha Kitt was in the first graduating class. That was 1948 and four years from high school, she was on Broadway. Al Pacino was a student here and Melissa Manchester, Dom de Luise, Liza Minelli . . .

(A young applicant carrying a small bag, RALPH GARCY, pauses to hear this.)

RALPH (interrupting). And Freddie. *Freddie Prinze*!

MRS. SHERWOOD (regretfully). Freddie didn't make it. He had to be expelled. A troublemaker.

RALPH. So cool, Freddie.

MRS. SHERWOOD (wryly). So cool.

RALPH. He came back in a Cadillac Eldorado — with a couple blondes hanging around his neck. Came back to let the old school take a good look at him.

MRS. SHERWOOD. I remember.

RALPH. They'll look up to me like that when I come out of here.

MRS. SHERWOOD. First you have to get in.

RALPH. I'll get in! (As he exits.) Freddie's old school.

MRS. SHERWOOD (seeing it again). Freddie double-parked his Eldorado in front of the school and there were blondes hanging around his neck alright! Then a few months later, he blew his own head off. (She considers.) Maybe if we hadn't been so hard on him . . . (The alternative.) . . . Or if we'd been a lot harder . . . (She takes a breath, then notices the other APPLICANTS.) For Al Pacino. For Liza Minelli. For all of them.

It begins with the same postcard: "Report at 9:30 a.m. Board of Education, City of New York. School of Performing Arts. West 46th Street."

(A group of GIRLS comes on.)

NICOLE. My legs are too short.

LISA (to MARIANNE). I love your scarf.

MARIANNE. It's my sister's.

JOY. I have a scene prepared.

MARIANNE. She went to high school here and she thought it would be good luck.

JOY. I mean a monologue.

NICOLE. I hate getting turned down. I really do.

JOY. I don't sing, though.

NICOLE. I know I could make it if I had a good body.

JOY. I'll die if they ask me to sing.

LISA. I'm really nervous. (The GIRLS begin to warm up.)

MRS. SHERWOOD. All girls . . . for the Dance Department. (A promise.) But there's a boy coming. As you see.

(LEROY JOHNSON, a tall, tough, semi-literate young man who moves with the natural grace of a born dancer, comes on L with an anxious, less graceful girl, SHIRLEY, who carries a handful of papers.)

MRS. SHERWOOD. Another boy asking to be expelled. Another troublemaker. (She is concerned.) Another chance for us to get him wrong — or get him right. (As LEROY and SHIRLEY approach her.) Names?

SHIRLEY. Excuse me, miss. You don't need his name. He's only my partner, see?

MRS. SHERWOOD. What school is he from?

SHIRLEY. He ain't into school. He's just helping me out, see, with my dancin' — he's just a partner. We've been rehearsing together, but it's me who's auditioning. Mullholland, see, Shirley, and I'm all fixed up. I filled in all your forms.

MRS. SHERWOOD (unmoved as SHIRLEY waves her handful of forms). He doesn't go past without giving me his name.

SHIRLEY (slowing down a little). Leroy's his name. But it's my audition. Shirley Mullholland. Two l's. (She confides.) Don't ask him to do any writing, miss. He gets real mean at that.

MRS. SHERWOOD. Doesn't he talk?

SHIRLEY. He ain't into conversation. Not till you know him.

MRS. SHERWOOD. Leroy what? (There is no reply.) If you want to audition . . . (She seems to have finally come to Leroy's attention.)

LEROY. I ain't come here for no *audition*! This my friend Shirley . . . She want to dance. I come here to help a friend, dass all. An' I ain't stayin' long.

MRS. SHERWOOD (correcting LEROY). You're not staying long.

SHIRLEY (quickly). Johnson. It's Leroy Johnson. Now can we go?

MRS. SHERWOOD (parting Leroy's jacket with her ruler, revealing a large hunting knife in a leather sheath). You're not staying at all unless you check your knife. (LEROY brushes Mrs. Sherwood's ruler aside.)

LEROY. You think I be's feeble or somethin'?

MRS. SHERWOOD (correcting LEROY). Am feeble.

LEROY. Man's gotta have a weapon.

MRS. SHERWOOD. You can pick up your weapon when you're finished.

LEROY. You kin pick up your head when I'm finished.

SHIRLEY. Leroy!

LEROY (to SHIRLEY). I ain't parkin' my blade with her little lame self!

SHIRLEY. She don't understand.

MRS. SHERWOOD. Speak English and I'll try harder.

LEROY. An' I'll try tap-dancin' on yo face right here and now!

MRS. SHERWOOD (eyeball to eyeball with LEROY). You're not dancing here or now until you check your knife. (SHIRLEY tugs at Leroy's sleeve. LEROY suddenly smiles dangerously at MRS. SHERWOOD. He whips out his knife.)

LEROY. You want it?

MRS. SHERWOOD (not flinching in the slightest). I want it.

LEROY. Shall I give it to you?

MRS. SHERWOOD (absolutely undaunted). Give it to me. (LEROY stares back but she is not going to give way. Suddenly, he breaks off this confrontation.)

LEROY. Promise you won't steal it? (He reverses the knife and hands it to MRS. SHERWOOD who gestures for LEROY and SHIRLEY to go R.)

SHIRLEY (to LEROY as she and LEROY go, relieved). Thanks, sugar.

LEROY. That's all right. (He opens his jacket for SHIRLEY to see his collection.) I got lotsa knives.

MRS. SHEROOD (as SHIRLEY and LEROY exit, considering the knife). That's how it started. That's the beginning.

(DORIS SCHWARTZ and MRS. SCHWARTZ enter L.)

MRS. SCHWARTZ (to DORIS). Don't be shy. Come with me. (She speaks sharply.) Doris . . .

MRS. SHERWOOD (addressing DORIS and MRS. SCHWARTZ). Can I help?

DORIS (holding up her postcard). I was told to report . . .

MRS. SCHWARTZ. Our audition.

MRS. SHERWOOD. Who are you?

MRS. SCHWARTZ (faintly irked). Her mother.

MRS. SHERWOOD (shaking her head). No . . .

MRS. SCHWARTZ. No what?

MRS. SHERWOOD. No mothers. (She starts DORIS and MRS. SCHWARTZ back L.) Please . . .

MRS. SCHWARTZ. She has a definite appointment. Doris, show her the postcard. (DORIS nervously holds up her postcard for MRS. SHERWOOD to see.)

MRS. SHERWOOD. Yes. That way. (As she goes.) You want to see Mr. Farrell. (As she exits, DORIS turns to MRS. SCHWARTZ.)

DORIS (burning with hushed embarrassment). I knew it! Just what I expected! *There are no other . . . mothers!*

MRS. SCHWARTZ (as if it were nonsense). Do you think I'd let you come without me?

DORIS. Am I a baby, stupid, not to be trusted out by myself? (She speaks bitterly.) And the way you made me dress . . . this is going to be the worst day of my entire life.

MRS. SCHWARTZ. We have to look our best. (She starts off.) Let's find this Mr. Farrell.

DORIS (as she is herded along). I look like Little Miss Muffet. All I need is a bowl of curds and whey . . . (As she and MRS. SCHWARTZ exit L.) And a spider.

(LYDIA comes on R, handing out numbers to DANCE APPLICANTS.)

LYDIA. Everyone needs a number.

MARIANNE (as ALL collect their numbers). Here we go! Countdown!

LISA. When I get nervous, my hair goes crazy.

NICOLE. The trouble is, I don't have a good body.

LISA. I sweat swimming pools.

JOY. I came here to dance. I don't want to sing, too.

MARIANNE. Performing arts. Dancing *and* acting . . . *and* singing.

JOY. Are we supposed to do everything?

(COCO enters.)

COCO (full of herself). It helps, baby. It sure helps!

JOY. Is that what you do?

COCO (emphatically agreeing). Me, I do everything! You wanta watch?

LISA (grudgingly, to COCO). I'll watch. (She is concerned.) My hair is definitely going crazy.

NICOLE. All my family has big bones. It's not my fault. (As LYDIA comes up to LEROY with a number.)

LEROY (bristling). You ain't puttin' no nuthin' on me! Stick yo number on you little self or give it to some fool what wants it! I ain't come here for no numbers. I ain't got time.

LYDIA (calmly). I love your watch.

LEROY (after a pause). I got lotsa watches.

SHIRLEY (to LEROY, irked at his interest in LYDIA). You be quiet.

LEROY. I ain't come here to be quiet. (To LYDIA.) I come here to dance, pretty mama.

LYDIA. What's your name?

LEROY. Joe.

LYDIA. Joe what?

LEROY. Joe Mama and Dad done made you bad.

SHIRLEY (cutting into this). How long we hafta wait?

LYDIA. You want to dance, you wait your chance.

LEROY. I ain't come here for no waitin'-in-line. I'm a working man. Shirley here . . . she wanna dance, dass fine.

(MISS BERG, the dance teacher, enters R.)

MISS BERG. May I have your attention, please.

LYDIA. The boss lady.

LEROY. She best hasten this line 'cause I ain't stayin' long.

MISS BERG. Thank you. Now the first thing I want you to do is just to walk across the floor so we can get a good look at you and see what your bodies are like. (She nods to the piano player, onstage or off, who starts a march, and ALL start off R.)

NICOLE. It's not fair.

LISA (grimly). Radioactivity hitting my hair.

JOY (to herself). Keep your head up. Smile.

MARIANNE (adjusting her scarf as she works herself well). Good luck, Marianne.

MISS BERG (to LYDIA as she follows the STUDENTS off). Just one boy.

LYDIA (as she follows off R). I don't know if he can pass English, but I bet he can dance.

MISS BERG (as she and LYDIA go off). What makes you so sure?

(We hear a voice reciting Shakespeare from off L. During this, MR. FARRELL enters L and crosses with his clipboard to sit in his folding chair.)

GIRL'S VOICE (off L). "Deny thy father and refuse thy name . . . or, if thou wilt not, be but sworn my love . . . and

I'll no longer be a Capulet." (She pronounces it "Cup-YOU-let.")

MR. FARRELL (calling to her). I'll have an upper classman read that with you.

(MICHAEL, handsome and a little older than the others, comes on L, leafing through a small book.)

MR. FARRELL. Michael . . . please. It's around page forty.
MICHAEL. Got it.

(DEIRDRE enters L.)

DEIRDRE. Shall I start from the beginning?
MR. FARRELL (betraying a little anxiety). That's not necessary. Just give Michael — Romeo — his cue.
DEIRDRE (clearing her throat). "And I'll no longer be a Cup-YOU-let."
MICHAEL (reading). "Shall I hear more, or shall I speak at this?" (He glances at MR. FARRELL who gestures for him to go on with it.)
DEIRDRE (butchering her lines). "Tis but thy name that is my enemy. Thou art thyself, though not a Montag." What's a Montag? "It is nor hand . . . (MICHAEL smothers a laugh, cut short by a gesture from MR. FARRELL.) . . . nor foot, nor arm, nor face . . . nor any part belonging to a man."
MR. FARRELL. Pardon me. It's Mon-tag-ue.
DEIRDRE. What?
MR. FARRELL (carefully). Mon. Tag. You. Not Montag. Okay?
DEIRDRE (smiling sweetly). Thank you. (She continues.) "Oh, be some other name." (She stops.) I forgot where I was.

MR. FARRELL. Just pick it up any place.

(DORIS enters L, pausing not to interrupt.)

DEIRDRE (after a slight pause). "What man art thou that thus bescreened in night so stumblest on my counsel?" (DORIS starts to retreat but is stopped by Michael's speech.)

MICHAEL (quickly as MR. FARRELL looks to him, reading very well). "By a name I know not how to tell thee who I am. My name, dear saint, is hateful to myself because it is an enemy to thee. Had I it written, I would tear the word." (DORIS is impressed by MICHAEL.)

MR. FARRELL (seeing DORIS). What is it?

DORIS (startled, embarrassed). Nothing. Sorry. (She gulps a breath, then refers to MICHAEL.) That was really . . .

MR. FARRELL (firmly). Wait with the others. (To MICHAEL.) Give her the cue. (To DEIRDRE.) Sorry.

MICHAEL (half playing to DORIS who pauses L). "Had I it written, I would tear the word." (A glance from MR. FAR-RELL sends DORIS off L.)

DEIRDRE. "Mine ears have not yet drunk a hundred words of thy tongue's uttering, yet I know the sound. Art thou not Romeo, and a Montag?" (MICHAEL laughs. She realizes.) I did it again. I'm sorry.

MR. FARRELL. No, we're sorry. This is the last day of auditions and we've seen three or four thousand students. It's late and we're a little punchy. I don't want that punchiness to penalize you. I want you to go next door and let Mrs. Shine audition you, alright? (DEIRDRE nods. He speaks kindly, before she starts off.) And it's Mon-tag-you.

DEIRDRE (as she goes off L, softly to herself). Mon . . . tag . . . you. Mon . . . tag . . . you.

(At R, a YOUNG MAN or a YOUNG GIRL comes on carrying
  a musical instrument, perhaps a flute or clarinet. The AP-
  PLICANT assumes a ready position. MR. FARRELL turns to
  MICHAEL.)

MR. FARRELL. You're a good actor, Michael. But if you laugh
  at someone's audition again, I'll flunk you. (The APPLICANT
  starts a brief musical passage.)
MICHAEL (subdued, to MR. FARRELL). Will you need me any-
  more today, Mr. Farrell?
MR. FARRELL (going L). Hang around.
MICHAEL (with mock humility, following MR. FARRELL off).
  Yes, sir.

(MR. SHOROFSKY, head of the Music Department, comes on,
  nodding appreciatively at the audition. He is a distinguished
  looking man — a former conductor of the Leipzig Symphony —
  as his students are unlikely to forget. DL, BRUNO MARTEL-
  LI, helped by his father ANGELO and his uncle MARIO,
  maneuvers a large synthesizer onto the stage.)

BRUNO (hopefully). Sounds like we're on the same floor with
  the Music Department.
ANGELO (to MARIO). Take it easy! That's seven thousand
  worth of machine!
MARIO. Dollars or pounds?
BRUNO. Don't touch the rotary pots.
MARIO. What pots? Nothing here but dials and switches.
BRUNO. On the V.C.O. (ALL push the synthesizer downstage
  of the APPLICANT and MR. SHOROFSKY.) I got it set on
  sawtooth.

(RALPH enters R and pauses to watch their approach.)

MARIO (to ANGELO). Why can't he play the piccolo or the accordion like Poppa did?

ANGELO. Same reason you drive a checker cab and not a Roman chariot, right? It's progress. My son's head is in the future. Besides, Poppa never could play the accordion.

BRUNO (to RALPH). Would you get the door, please?

(COCO comes on R.)

RALPH. My number is next. The biggie.

COCO. I'll get the door.

BRUNO. Thanks.

ANGELO. Some load.

RALPH. What is it?

COCO. That's an ARP . . . AXXE. (As BRUNO, ANGELO and MARIO follow her off R.)

BRUNO (admiringly). Right. (RALPH looks after them. The APPLICANT finishes.)

MR. SHOROFSKY. Thank you. You play very good. (As the APPLICANT smiles with pleasure.) Do you like the violin? (The APPLICANT is nervous at the question. He explains.) We're short on strings. Never mind. (He makes a check on the clipboard.) Thank you. (As the APPLICANT exits, he calls.) Next. (RALPH freezes for an instant.)

RALPH (repeating). Next.

(COCO enters and gives RALPH a little shove.)

COCO. The man said — next. (RALPH runs down to stand in front of MR. SHOROFSKY. COCO stays on R to watch.)

RALPH (the good news here). I'm — next!

MR. SHOROFSKY. What's your name?

RALPH. Ralph Garcy.

MR. SHOROFSKY. Would you move back a little. (As RALPH takes a very small step back.) Who taught you?

RALPH. My father. (MR. SHOROFSKY just looks at him. RALPH doesn't trust silences and he quickly continues.) He's doing work for the government now. I'm not supposed to talk about him. But he was very famous. He played in symphonies all over the world. Once.

MR. SHOROFSKY. What did he play?

RALPH. Guitars. (Another silence, so he improvises.) And horns. French horns. (Silence.) And English horns. (Silence.) And trumpets.

MR. SHOROFSKY. Anything else?

RALPH. Violins.

MR. SHOROFSKY (cautiously). And what did he teach you? (RALPH reaches deep into his pocket and pulls out a cheap harmonica, waving it proudly.)

RALPH. Are you ready? (Ignoring Mr. Shorofsky's wince, he launches into a very bad but very enthusiastic cacophany. MR. SHOROFSKY raises his hand to stop him but he considers himself on a roll and he's hard to stop.)

MR. SHOROFSKY (bellowing). *Thank you*! (RALPH gives it one last off-key wail and stops. MR. SHOROFSKY speaks quietly.) Thank you. (As RALPH waits for the good news.) Tell me. Do you like to dance?

RALPH (with a big grin). *Love* to dance!

MR. SHOROFSKY. Then why don't you try the Dance Department? (He calls ahead to someone off R as he heads in that direction.) I'm taking a short break.

RALPH (to COCO who has been watching impassively). I guess he figures I can do anything.

COCO. Figures something, all right. Would you like a suggestion?

RALPH (as he exits). Save it.

COCO (looking after RALPH as he goes past). I gotta enough to spare. (Smiling, she goes off after RALPH.)

(MRS. SCHWARTZ follows MR. FARRELL on. They are followed by DORIS.)

MRS. SCHWARTZ. We know our rights. You can't refuse her an audition.

MR. FARRELL (tiredly). No problem. I'll hear her.

MRS. SCHWARTZ. If she can have an accompanist . . . (She speaks quickly, holding up a small cassette player.) But if she can't, I brought this.

MR. FARRELL. She's not supposed to sing her audition. You were told that. This is the Drama Department.

MRS. SCHWARTZ (emphatically). When she sings, it *is* drama.

DORIS (hushed, a plea). Mother . . .

MRS. SCHWARTZ (insisting). *It is drama*! (MR. FARRELL pauses, then looks at DORIS who seems to be only interested in the floor.)

MR. FARRELL (gently, calling across to DORIS). What's your name?

MRS. SCHWARTZ. Schwartz. (MR. FARRELL looks at her.) Doris. Doris Schwartz.

MR. FARRELL (to DORIS). Who taught you? (DORIS opens her mouth to answer but she isn't fast enough.)

MRS. SCHWARTZ. Barbra Streisand. (DORIS is mortally embarrassed, but MRS. SCHWARTZ won't stop.) She has all her records. She saw *A Star is Born* fourteen times.

DORIS (finally). Five. And a half. On Home Box Office.

MRS. SCHWARTZ. And I do what I can. Of course.

MR. FARRELL (to DORIS). How's that?

DORIS (softly). Mama pays for my singing lessons. And sends me on commercial auditions.

MR. FARRELL. I can't hear you.

DORIS (murmuring). I'm sorry.

MR. FARRELL. What?

MRS. SCHWARTZ (half yelling). She's sorry. (MR. FARRELL turns toward MRS. SCHWARTZ again.) She's a little nervous.

MR. FARRELL (talking off L). Michael . . .

MRS. SCHWARTZ (adding). But not when she sings.

(MICHAEL enters and waits for MR. FARRELL who crosses to DORIS.)

MR. FARRELL (gently, to DORIS). Why do you want to go to school here, Doris?

DORIS. To be an actress. A good actress. A good, serious actress. And . . . (She hesitates, looking at MRS. SCHWARTZ.)

MR. FARRELL. What?

DORIS (quietly). We can't afford a professional school.

MRS. SCHWARTZ. Speak up, Doris. (MR. FARRELL takes DORIS by the hand.)

MR. FARRELL. Do you want to sing now?

DORIS. I'm a little nervous.

MR. FARRELL (to MICHAEL). Stand over here. (He is softly emphatic.) And you give her support.

DORIS (confused). What am I to do?

MR. FARRELL (introducing). Michael — this is Doris. She's going to sing to you. (To DORIS.) Look at Michael — and sing to him. Don't worry about anything or anyone else.

DORIS. I don't think I can do that. I can't just . . . stare.

MR. FARRELL. Think of it as a concentration exercise, alright?

(He pauses. DORIS is still uncertain.) He won't mind. (To MICHAEL.) Will you? (MICHAEL turns to DORIS and gives her a radiant smile. DORIS takes this in nervously. To MRS. SCHWARTZ.) *Now* you can do something useful . . . (MRS. SCHWARTZ is ready!) Start the accompaniment.

MRS. SCHWARTZ. Right! (She starts the player and steps back to watch the triumph. MICHAEL nods encouragingly to DORIS who begins to sing *The Way We Were*.)

DORIS (singing in a small, sweet, nervous voice). "Memries light the corners of my mind, Misty water color memries, Of the way we were . . ."

MR. FARRELL (only to MICHAEL, quietly). Keep smiling. (DORIS forces herself to focus on MICHAEL who smiles back relentlessly. With the lyrics, DORIS begins a small smile in return.)

DORIS (singing). "Scattered pictures of the smiles we left behind, Smiles we gave to one another, For the way we were." (MRS. SCHWARTZ is feeling great emotion as she watches. She takes out an instamatic camera and takes a flash picture of DORIS as she sings. The explosion of the flashbulb takes DORIS by surprise and makes her hesitate. MR. FARRELL, concerned for the girl, crosses to DORIS.)

MR. FARRELL. Go on. (As DORIS hesitates, he reaches down and turns off the cassette player, then repeats.) Go on . . .

DORIS (confused). But . . .

MR. FARRELL. Speak the lyrics. (As DORIS tries to get hold of this.) To Michael . . . (MICHAEL encourages DORIS, speaking a line from the lyrics.)

MICHAEL. "Can it be that it was all so simple then, Or has time rewritten evry line?" (With a little burst of hope, DORIS picks up speaking the lyrics. Her eyes remain locked on Michael's as she recites the story of loneliness and lost love.)

DORIS (picking up the next line, getting connected). "If we had

the chance to do it all again. Tell me, would we? Could we?"
(MR. FARRELL watches with increasing interest. DORIS de-
livers the words of the song with conviction.) "Memries may be
beautiful and yet, What's too painful to remember, We simply
choose to forget." (She seems taller now and her eyes shine
from within.) "So it's the laughter, We will remember, Whenever we remember, The way we were."

MICHAEL. "The way we were."

DORIS. "The way we were." (As she finishes, MRS.
SCHWARTZ breaks into noisy applause.)

MR. FARRELL. That was very nice. Thank you. (MRS.
SCHWARTZ wipes her eyes with a handkerchief. MR. FAR-
RELL makes a slight gesture off L.) Very nice. (DORIS under-
stands and starts off. After her.) Oh, Doris. (DORIS
turns to look at him. As though an afterthought.) What would
you do if you don't make it?

MRS. SCHWARTZ (grimly emphatic). *We'll make it*! (She takes
Doris' hand. As she and DORIS march off.) We'll make it!
(MR. FARRELL sits in his chair and starts making notes on his
clipboard.)

MICHAEL (turning to MR. FARRELL, curiously). Did she make
it?

MR. FARRELL (without looking up). The mother or the
daughter? (MICHAEL shrugs and exits as MR. FARRELL continues with his notes.)

(BRUNO, MARIO and ANGELO enter UR, maneuvering the
synthesizer along. MARIO and ANGELO give BRUNO an
encouraging slap and gesture, then go off R. BRUNO quickly
starts to make adjustments on the machine. As he is doing so,
COCO and RALPH enter DR. COCO suppresses laughter at
what she has just seen.)

COCO (calling to RALPH). Hey, man . . .

RALPH. Pretty good audition, huh?

COCO (incredulously). You mean dancin' a jerky time-step to *Swanee River*? (She "dum-dum-de-dums" the music to *Swanee River* as she imitates RALPH doing his time-step.)

RALPH (defensively). They told me to try the Drama Department. They figure I can do it all, right?

COCO. That's not what they're telling you. (She does a quick, precise modern dance turn.) *I* can do it all.

RALPH (sarcastically). How about house seats for when your show opens?

COCO. Listen . . . (Confidentially.) Nobody talks about it, but there's a quota system. Your chances are better if you're black or Puerto Rican — or a little bit of everything. Like me. (RALPH starts to make a sarcastic reply but then stops himself. Maybe she's right.)

RALPH (after a beat). I *am* Puerto Rican.

COCO (scoffing). Not on paper you're not. (She puts his phony name in quotes.) "Ralph Garcy." And all that noise about your daddy doin' work for the government.

RALPH (hotly). That's the truth.

COCO. Sure. And he was famous. World famous! (She quotes.) "My father danced with all the Rockettes!"

RALPH (starting). That's . . .

COCO (scornfully). The *Rockettes*? (Then seriously.) You only get one more chance, baby. Better tell 'em the truth this time.

RALPH (meaning "I got that"). Thank you.

MR. FARRELL (calling). Next.

RALPH (calling back). I'm next! (COCO gives him a "thumb's up" and goes as he walks UL to stand before MR. FARRELL.)

MR. FARRELL. What's your name?

RALPH (hesitating, then speaking tentatively). Raul. Raul Garcia.

MR. FARRELL. Where are you from?

RALPH. San Juan. Once. I came here when I was a baby. I grew up in the South Bronx.

MR. FARRELL. Who taught you?

RALPH. My father. (He gets back into his groove.) He's in Spain right now making Italian westerns.

MR. FARRELL. Uh-huh.

RALPH (getting off it). But that's not the point.

MR. FARRELL. Why do you want to go to school here?

RALPH (quietly serious). Freddie went here.

MR. FARRELL. Freddie?

RALPH. Freddie Prinze. He was the best.

MR. FARRELL. You want to be an actor.

RALPH (doing a terrible imitation of Cary Grant). "Judy, Judy, Judy . . ." (He squares his shoulders in a James Cagney impression.) "Top of the world, Ma."

MR. FARRELL (hiding his irritation). Can that. I don't want you to perform. I want to see who *you* are. Do you understand?

RALPH (uncertainly). Sure.

MR. FARRELL. Use your own experience. Be simple. Be honest. But most of all be yourself.

RALPH (betting it all). I can perform! I'll do a scene. (He throws off his coat, pulls a chair over to himself, and stands on it, standing as tall as he can.) I'm God, see? And I'm talking to this angel, giving him the business of the day. That's why I'm standing on this chair because I'm God. And God is Puerto Rican and He works in a steambath, see . . . and the angel is a computer, an electronic computer. (BRUNO, his equipment connected, begins to warm up. This acts as an underscoring for RALPH. *Note: If the actor playing the role of Bruno is not also a musician who can handle a synthesizer effectively, it is possible to use a recording with the actor miming his playing.*)

RALPH. Hiya, baby . . . San Diego Freeway. I'm still God, right? All right, first thing I want that Pontiac moving south past Hermosa Beach to crash into the light blue Eldorado coming the other way. Make it a head-on collision. *No survivors*! (Bruno's music gives this a quick wrap up. MR. FARRELL laughs.)

MR. FARRELL. I didn't expect Friedman's *Steambath.*

RALPH (getting off the chair, frankly). I didn't expect I'd remember! (He is quietly determined.) I gotta get into Freddie's school.

MR. FARRELL (meeting this with frank sincerity). This isn't a school for the Freddie Prinzes. Performing Arts means hard work; discipline − not showboating and pyrotechnics.

RALPH (sharply). Give it to me? Am I in or out?

MR. FARRELL (considering). I'm not sure which would be doing you the bigger favor.

RALPH (in a moment of fear). There's no other department for me to try.

MR. FARRELL. You'll hear. Like the others. Thank you, Mr. Garcia. (Sensing rejection, RALPH grabs his coat and goes off L, accompanied by another riff from BRUNO at the synthesizer.)

(As the riff subsides, MR. SHOROFSKY comes in R, curious as to what is going on.)

MR. SHOROFSKY. What is . . . (He stops to consider the machine, then speaks to BRUNO.) Do you need a license to operate that thing?

BRUNO. What?

MR. SHOROFSKY. I mean, do you want to be a musician or an
airline pilot?

BRUNO (a statement of fact). I'm a musician.

MR. SHOROFSKY. Okay, Mr. . . . (He looks at his clipboard
as he seats himself.) Mr. Martelli. We're ready when you are.
(BRUNO nods, then begins. Out of the speakers comes a
swelling flood of orchestral sounds — strings, horns, reeds,
percussion. The synthesizer is working an electronic miracle.
He is surprised.) Mr. Martelli . . . (BRUNO is lost in his
music and doesn't hear.) Mr. Martelli! (BRUNO bends his
head closer to the roar of instruments.) *Mr. Martelli!*
(BRUNO stops and looks up expectantly.) One instrument at
a time will be sufficient. (BRUNO is surprised. He shrugs and
begins to turn off the switches.)

BRUNO. I can do it in five four if you prefer it with a disco beat.

MR. SHOROFSKY. That won't be necessary. (He goes to
BRUNO with a sheet of music.) But you have to take the sight
reading test. That's obligatory.

BRUNO. If that's what you need . . . (He begins to play the
music accurately and with casual ease. MR. SHOROFSKY
stops him.)

MR. SHOROFSKY (faintly irritated). Fine. That's enough.
(He is suspicious.) Are you sure you haven't studied that piece
before?

BRUNO. Maybe I heard it. My father's into that kind of stuff.

MR. SHOROFSKY. What kind of stuff?

BRUNO. Moldy oldies.

MR. SHOROFSKY. I beg your pardon?

BRUNO. Bach. Mozart. Puccini . . . (He gestures.) All those
old guys.

MR. SHOROFSKY. You just dismissed four centuries of classical
music . . . (He imitates Bruno's gesture.) With that.

BRUNO. Do you want to hear some real music? (He clicks switches and turns dials.)

MR. SHOROFSKY (quickly). No. I'm through for the day. You're my last audition. (BRUNO starts to play music with a disco beat.)

BRUNO. Do you mind if I –

MR. SHOROFSKY. They'll hear this in the Dance Department.

(DANCE APPLICANTS, LYDIA and MISS BERG come on upstage.)

MR. SHOROFSKY (conceding). Maybe they'll like this in the Dance Department. (COCO emerges from the other APPLICANTS, dancing to the synthesizer.)

BRUNO (challenging MR. SHOROFSKY). What about *you*?

MR. SHOROFSKY. I'm sorry to say – you're very talented. (As he goes.) But I'll pay you back for this headache when I get you into music theory class.

BRUNO (as what MR. SHOROFSKY says sinks in, half to himself). When you get me into music theory class . . . (Realizing that he's made it, he brings up the volume on the synthesizer. MR. SHOROFSKY is driven off R by the mounting decibels.)

MR. SHOROFSKY (shouting back over the sound as he goes). Where you'll spend four years with Mozart . . . Vivaldi . . . and the rest of those old guys. (Lost in his music, BRUNO keeps playing. The sound reaches ALL in the Dance Department, some of whom make small moves with it, though not as flamboyantly as COCO.)

MISS BERG (stopping COCO). You've already had your turn. (To LYDIA.) Who's next?

LYDIA (calling out). Number eighty.

SHIRLEY (to LEROY, in panic). That's us.

LYDIA. Number eighty.

SHIRLEY (coming forward). Shirley Mullholland . . . and my partner.

MISS BERG (to LYDIA). The boy?

LYDIA (with the list). Leroy Johnson.

MISS BERG (to SHIRLEY). What music?

SHIRLEY. I brought a cassette . . .

LEROY (beginning to move to what we're hearing). Dass all right. I relate to what's comin' through the wall.

MISS BERG. Up to you.

SHIRLEY (worried). Leroy . . .

MISS BERG. Five, six, seven, eight . . . (LEROY is into the dance with SHIRLEY trying to get into it too. While BRUNO is unaware of them, his music is strong support. From casual interest, the OTHERS become an audience. LEROY tries to bring SHIRLEY into what he's doing but she's increasingly out of it. LEROY gives up with SHIRLEY and lets the music take him up solo. He loves the attention and begins to lay some funky moves on all the admiring chicks as MISS BERG speaks to LYDIA.) The poor girl is a disaster . . .

LYDIA. I had a feeling the boy could dance.

MISS BERG (as she looks through the forms). Where's his application?

LYDIA. He doesn't have one. He's with her. (She and MISS BERG look at SHIRLEY who is beginning to give up.)

MISS BERG. Get him an application.

LYDIA. He's a mistake.

MISS BERG (emphatically). He's a boy and he dances. Get him an application. (LEROY feels cool, together, and higher than he's ever been. He could dance here forever. SHIRLEY is defeated and miserable, aware that the total focus is on LEROY. She stops dancing and moves to the side, glowering in anger and pain. LEROY does his moves for his admirers as MISS BERG speaks in an aside to LYDIA.) What do you call that?

LYDIA (smiling as she watches LEROY). Wicked. (SHIRLEY can't stand it any longer. She picks up her cassette player and walks C, interrupting.)

SHIRLEY. Stop! *Stop*! (She holds up the cassette player.) We have to start over — with the right music! Like it was rehearsed!

MISS BERG. That won't be necessary.

SHIRLEY. It's necessary!

MISS BERG. Thank you, Miss Mullholland.

SHIRLEY (repeating softly). Thank you? (Bruno's music swells and LEROY, caught by it, does a final turn. He freezes in this position, the music climaxes, and the lights blackout except for a spot on LEROY. In this sudden moment of quiet, LEROY starts bringing himself back to reality. SHIRLEY, now subdued, comes into the spot of light. The OTHERS are in darkness and then gone.) You're not into high school, remember?

LEROY (shrugging). I'm thinkin' about it. Anyway, I'm into dancin'.

SHIRLEY (with a short, sour laugh). You're into chicks, you mean. You don't have to go to no high school for that. Who asked you to work my audition anyway?

LEROY. You did. I was doin' you a favor, remember?

SHIRLEY (her lips trembling). Some fat favor! (LYDIA approaches them, carrying some forms.)

LYDIA (to LEROY). Fill out these forms and give them to the senior at the door to the Dance Department.

SHIRLEY. And me?

LYDIA. You can wait for him on one of the chairs at the back.

SHIRLEY (as she gets what has been said). I'm through. (Her

unhappiness grows.) I didn't make it . . . Thank you . . .
Right? (LYDIA has no answer. A new thought grows in
SHIRLEY.) Why does he have to go fill out forms? Why's he
hafta give them to the Dance Department? (LYDIA gestures
off R to LEROY.) I get it. You think I'm stupid or some-
thing? He's in and I'm out, right? I get a ticket home, right?
LEROY. Gotta go . . . (LYDIA starts off R.)
SHIRLEY. The hell with you, Leroy! This was my audition. We
was rehearsin' to get *me* into this school, not *you*! It's not fair.
(LEROY starts off into the darkness R.) You stupid bastard!
(She shouts after LEROY.) You can't make it in school anyway! You'll fail — you'll flunk! Flunk out! (LEROY is gone.
She calls into the empty darkness.) I didn't want to come here
anyway. You done me a favor, Leroy, you louse. You gone
and saved me four long years at this dumbass school! (There is
no one to hear and the tears come. She speaks with a smother-
ed sob.) You're looking at one happy lady! (She walks off into
the darkness L as she speaks.) One happy lady.

(MRS. SHERWOOD walks into the center of the spot of light.)

MRS. SHERWOOD. The bad news for that girl was so quick it
was merciful. The good news for Doris Schwartz didn't reach
her directly.

(MRS. SCHWARTZ comes into the light upstage, holding a
phone.)

MRS. SCHWARTZ (into the phone, with anxious intensity).
Yes? Yes? *Yes*?
MRS. SHERWOOD. She finds out in the usual way . . .
MRS. SCHWARTZ (gasping, turning, shouting with all her
strength). Doris — *we're in*!

MRS. SHERWOOD.   And a few others assigned to my homeroom. (MRS. SCHWARTZ goes off.)

(The lights come up and we see a semblance of a CLASS sitting
in chair desks that they've brought while the rest of the stage
was dark. MRS. SHERWOOD crosses to her own desk, calling
out as she crosses.)

MRS. SHERWOOD. Martelli, Bruno.

BRUNO. Here.

MRS. SHERWOOD. Hernandez, Coco.

COCO. Here.

MRS. SHERWOOD. Garcia, Raul. (There is no answer. She calls
in a louder voice.) Garcia, Raul.

RALPH. It's Ralph.

MRS. SHERWOOD. It says Raul.

COCO (with fun, not malice). Yeah, but he don't relate to that.

RALPH. Thank you.

MRS. SHERWOOD. Garcia, Ralph.

RALPH. Garcy. (The OTHERS laugh.) I been goin' through
some changes.

MRS. SHERWOOD (correcting the card). Garcy, Ralph.

RALPH (loudly). All right!

MRS. SHERWOOD. MacNeill, Montgomery.

MONTGOMERY. Here.

MRS. SHERWOOD. Gustafson, Lisa.

LISA. Present.

MRS. SHERWOOD. Allen, Nicole. (NICOLE is almost taken un-
awares, putting some finishing touches on her makeup. She
looks up suddenly.)

NICOLE. Yes?

MRS. SHERWOOD. Johnson, Leroy. (There is no answer. She

looks up, then speaks louder.) Johnson, Leroy! (She walks over to LEROY who sits with his eyes shut and his radio headset on. She turns the dial sharply. LEROY jumps up, startled.) Check your radio.

LEROY. Hey!

MRS. SHERWOOD. It doesn't belong in a classroom. In the future, Mr. Johnson, leave your ghetto blaster at home.

LEROY. I brought it in the event of bein' bored. An' I done been bored . . . (Under his breath to the OTHERS.) Since evah I saw her evil face.

MRS. SHERWOOD (stung by the titters from the CLASS). You're going to see this same evil face for the next four years, Mr. Johnson. You're going to be in this same room at the right time every single school day with your home-work done, your eyes open, your mouth shut, your pencil sharpened and all food, cigarettes and radios outside. Those are the rules of this homeroom, Mr. Johnson, and you'll either get used to them — or get out.

LEROY. Ain't nobody makin' me walk 'less I wants to walk.

MRS. SHERWOOD. Why *are* you here, Mr. Johnson?

LEROY (lighting up). 'Cause I's young and single an' I loves to mingle.

MRS. SHERWOOD. Speak English.

LEROY. I speaks like I likes.

MRS. SHERWOOD. This is my homeroom. You'll speak as I like. I teach English. If that's a foreign language, you'll learn it. (She moves around the room, addressing the OTHERS.) This is no Mickey Mouse school. You're not getting off easy because you're talented. I don't care how cute you are . . . or how well you dance . . . If you don't give your academic subjects equal time — you're out. (She walks back to her desk.) There will be a new word on the blackboard every day. We'll define it and then you'll use it in a sentence. The word for today is — tyranny. A government in which absolute power is vested in a single ruler . . . the office, authority or administration of such a ruler. (There are muffled groans and a barely stiffled curse from LEROY. MRS. SHERWOOD can tell that they're getting the message. The light comes down to a spot again. The CLASS MEMBERS exit with their chair desks. MRS. SHERWOOD comes DC into the spot.) The difference between the High School of Performing Arts and other high schools is that at P.A. you spend half your day working in your department — drama, music or dance. The other half of the day is for academic subjects — and the third half is spent practicing, rehearsing, practicing exercises and more practicing. That gives you three halves which is impossible and that doesn't include homework, term papers, exams, studying or working up presentations to perform in class. (She starts out of the light.) That doesn't leave more than fifteen minutes for home life — or anything else. (She goes off.)

(MR. FARRELL comes into the light as MRS. SHERWOOD goes.)

MR. FARRELL. Acting is the hardest profession in the world. My agent once told me that he could put his fingers on fifty thousand people who call themselves actors and maybe five hundred of whom make a living acting. And most of those do commercials to pay the rent. The rest wait tables, clean apartments — and live off welfare and hope.

(The lights come up to reveal the STUDENTS seated in a semi-circle listening.)

MR. FARRELL. You'll have to have a solid technique, a good agent, and most of all a thick skin because you're part of an underprivileged minority. You're going to have to suffer cattle calls, rejection, humiliation. For every job there are hundreds of smiling resumes thrown in the basket. (RALPH notices DORIS and sits beside her.) And you better like yourself a lot because that's all you've got to work with. Use yourself. Your voice. Your experience.

RALPH (putting his arm around DORIS, in a half whisper). You wanna accumulate some experience? (DORIS pulls away.) I got experience to spare.

MR. FARRELL. You have to find out who you are and use your experiences to create honest moments onstage.

RALPH (half whispering to DORIS). I live with two chicks. (DORIS stares down at the floor.) That's a dynamite floor. (DORIS moves away as the lights on this scene dim.)

MR. FARRELL. Start being aware of your feelings — so you can draw on them when necessary.

(Light comes up at R where MR. SHOROFSKY lectures to his STUDENTS.)

MR. SHOROFSKY. We have not enough violins, so everyone must minor in strings. This is so we have good orchestras for assemblies and concerts. And then you have sight-singing, keyboard harmony, elementary piano, and then you have music history, orchestration, dance band —

COCO. When do we have lunch?

MR. SHOROFSKY (with no humor). Eleven-thirty. One-half hour. And then you have everything else.

BRUNO. What's everything else?

MR. SHOROFSKY. Biology, chemistry, algebra, English, history —

COCO. Do we get to sleep?

MR. SHOROFSKY (sighing). Too much sleep is not good for artists. Do you love music? You must give up something. (The light on him begins to dim as it comes up L.) Music is the hardest profession in the world.

(MISS BERG comes into the light at L with her DANCERS in a semi-circle.)

MISS BERG. Dance is the hardest department in the school. You have to arrive earlier to get dressed and warmed up. You'll have to take outside classes in your major field and study ballet, modern, folk, tap, jazz and historical dance here. Not to mention dance history, supported adagio variation class, make-up, hairstyling, even acting for dancers.

LEROY (muttering). Let's cut the mumbo jumbo and turn on the music.

MISS BERG (ignoring LEROY). In addition to dealing with the usual dancers' complaints . . . pulled tendons, skin splints and swollen toes. Dancing isn't a way of getting through school. It's a way of life *plus* school. And the school part is easier. You can fail French or geometry and make it up at night. But if you flunk a dance class, you're out. Any questions?

PHENICIA. I came here to express the exploitation of under-privileged minorities through the medium of modern dance.

MISS BERG. I'm sure you did. What's your question?

PHENICIA. What do I need with a decadent racist art form?

MISS BERG. You mean ballet?

PHENICIA. Yes.

MISS BERG. Four years. Anything else? (LEROY raises his hand.) Yes?

LEROY. These tights you be talkin' about —

MISS BERG. What about tights?

LEROY. I ain't wearin' 'em. An' I ain't havin' to be here for no warmin' up early. I be warmed up, woman, twenty-five hours a day. I'm hot around the clock.

MISS BERG (to LEROY). It isn't enough.

LEROY (puzzled). What?

MISS BERG. Twenty-five hours a day. (To the GROUP.) You all want fame. Well, fame costs. (She starts away from the STUDENTS, then pauses for a last, hard shot.) And right here is where you start paying.

(Music comes up and the STUDENTS start energetic practice. DORIS comes on DL, stops, puts down her books, takes out a mirror and starts a critical inspection of her face. MONT-GOMERY comes up to DORIS and tries for her attention. Behind them, the dance practice continues to heat up.)

MONTGOMERY. Hi . . . (As DORIS sees him.) I'm in your acting class. (He holds out his hand.) Montgomery MacNeill.

DORIS (as she shakes hands gravely). Doris Schwartz. Isn't your mother Marsha MacNeill? The actress?

MONTGOMERY. That's right. Yes.

DORIS. She does wonderful work.

MONTGOMERY (with pleasure). Have you seen her?

DORIS. Not really. But I've heard. I didn't know she lived in New York.

MONTGOMERY. She doesn't. Well, officially she does, but

she's on the road forever. She gets paid to stay in hotels, but she stays with friends so her per diems all come home to me and Doctor Golden.

DORIS. Is Doctor Golden your stepfather?

MONTGOMERY. No, my analyst.

DORIS (curiously). What's wrong with you?

MONTGOMERY. I have problems.

DORIS (hesitantly). Oh. Well, I have problems, too.

MONTGOMERY. There's *nothing* wrong with you.

DORIS. You don't understand. *That's* what's wrong with me. Everybody else here is eccentric or colorful or charismatic. And I'm perfectly ordinary. My body is ordinary. I don't know why I'm here.

MONTGOMERY. You want to be an actress.

DORIS. Actors and actresses are flamboyant, colorful beings. I'm about as flamboyant as . . . as . . . as a bagel.

(MICHAEL, with several admiring GIRLS, enters. He smiles at DORIS as he passes.)

MONTGOMERY. Some people like bagels.

DORIS. And some people don't like bagels.

MONTGOMERY. Some people are too old for you.

DORIS (defensively). He helped me get into the school. I sang and talked to him at my audition. And he smiled at me.

MONTGOMERY. He smiles at everyone.

DORIS. And he winks.

MONTGOMERY. I think that's a nervous habit.

DORIS. And he talks to me. Often.

MONTGOMERY. What does he say?

DORIS. Hi.

MONTGOMERY (lightly). Oh, well. That's serious. Have you

set the date? (Hurt, DORIS turns away.) I'm sorry.

DORIS. I feel stupid.

MONTGOMERY (briskly). Get into it. Study it . . . as an acting exercise. The feeling of stupidity. So you can remember it and reproduce it.

DORIS. Thanks.

MONTGOMERY (hesitating). Would you like to share my locker?

(RALPH enters and approaches DORIS and MONTGOMERY.)

DORIS (shyly). Yes.

RALPH. Hello, M and M. You seen your shrink lately?

MONTGOMERY. Yesterday.

RALPH (curiously). What's going on? Can't be anything serious . . . (He pats Montgomery's shoulder.) Not with little Montgomery here!

DORIS. What?

RALPH. Oops — shut mah mouth. (He dances away.)

DORIS (gritting her teeth, with disgust). I *hate* Ralph Garcy. I really do. (She realizes something important.) I must remember this feeling. (She starts off. MONTGOMERY follows.)

MONTGOMERY. You're right. Use it in your acting. (A bell rings. The music and dance practice stops. Some of the STUDENTS bring their chair desks to set up the English class.) Homeroom. (He and DORIS go off.)

(MONTGOMERY and DORIS return with their chair desks and join the OTHERS in setting up the class. MRS. SHERWOOD enters DR and crosses L, then pauses. She walks into the class and goes up to where LEROY is sitting.)

MRS. SHERWOOD. Mr. Johnson? (LEROY stares ahead without looking up at her.) What about your homework?

LEROY. I forgot it.

MRS. SHERWOOD. For two weeks?

LEROY (loudly). I told you I done it and I forgot it.

MRS. SHERWOOD. My hearing's fine. It's your homework that's missing. And the quality of the page that I have is unsatisfactory.

LEROY. The quality of yo face is unsatisfactory.

MRS. SHERWOOD. I'm not here to trade insults, Mr. Johnson.

LEROY. That page is in a secret language. It's not meant for bigots to understand.

MRS. SHERWOOD. This isn't a joke.

LEROY. I got lotsa jokes.

MRS. SHERWOOD. This is garbage.

LEROY. My pen broke.

MRS. SHERWOOD. It's in pencil. (Nervous laughter ripples through the class.)

LEROY. That broke, too.

MRS. SHERWOOD. Listen carefully. (She is deliberately emphatic.) If you can't learn to read, you can't learn to dance. You're flunking out.

LEROY (stung). I can read.

MRS. SHERWOOD. Yes?

LEROY (a little less loudly). I can read. (MRS. SHERWOOD steps back to her desk, picks up a book, then comes back.)

MRS. SHERWOOD (opening the book and putting it in front of LEROY). Then read.

LEROY. No.

MRS. SHERWOOD. *Read this*!

DORIS (nervously intervening). Mrs. Sherwood . . .

MRS. SHERWOOD (snapping). What is it?

DORIS (indicating the book). That's *Silas Marner*. (She tries to smile.) Nobody relates to *Silas Marner*. (She quickly leafs through a book of her own.) There's a really good passage in this – *To Kill a Mockingbird*.

MRS. SHERWOOD (taking a beat). You've got a point. (DORIS hands over the book for MRS. SHERWOOD to consider.)

LEROY. I won't read that either. No way!

MRS. SHERWOOD. Study it for a minute. It's very good. Then . . .

LEROY. No!

MRS. SHERWOOD. Read! (Desperately, LEROY springs out of his seat and, in a fury, goes to the door where he stops and turns. The STUDENTS, startled, stand up.)

LEROY (screaming). I can read, you bigot! Damn you – I can read! (With a cry, he races off. MRS. SHERWOOD trembles.)

MRS. SHERWOOD. Wait . . .

DORIS (calling). Leroy . . .

(There are yells and the smashing of glass heard from the direction of Leroy's exit. The lights dim and ALL exit as the sounds of the city come up. LEROY comes on DR, alone in the only light on the stage. He suppresses a sob.)

LEROY. Bigot . . . Hassle City . . . Down on me since day one!

(DORIS comes onstage into another pool of light DL.)

DORIS. Leroy . . . hey!

(MICHAEL comes onstage UR.)

MICHAEL (registering on DORIS and LEROY). What is this . . . a field trip? (LEROY whirls around with his back to MICHAEL and DORIS.) What's wrong with him?

DORIS (subdued). He forgot his homework.

MICHAEL. No more homework for me.

DORIS. You won the scholarship. You *are* the best actor in the school.

MICHAEL. Your name is . . .

DORIS. Doris. Doris Schwartz. (She takes a breath.) You remember?

MICHAEL. Oh, sure. Right.

DORIS (uncertainly). Yeah . . . Have you decided where you're going?

MICHAEL. California.

DORIS. I meant college. Your scholarship.

MICHAEL. I can't use it. William Morris has big plans for me.

DORIS. The biggest agent!

MICHAEL. A couple of series they think I'm right for. (He smiles.) I'm off into the sunset . . . (He cocks a finger at DORIS like a pistol.) See you in Hollywood . . . (He goes off into the darkness.)

DORIS (after MICHAEL). Good luck . . . (She corrects herself.) Break a leg! (She takes a breath, feeling a fool. Then she sees LEROY. It's so ridiculous.) His smile got me through my audition, got me into the school.

LEROY. I flunk out, I'll get me an agent.

DORIS (considering LEROY). You can read.

LEROY. You wanta hassle me, too? (Angry, he starts tearing up a piece of paper he's holding.)

DORIS (starting slowly towards LEROY). We all want to be in the theatre. Well, we're supposed to help each other. (She looks after MICHAEL.) I got help . . . and he doesn't even remember my name . . .

LEROY. What d'ya want?

DORIS. What's on the piece of paper? (As LEROY looks at the scrap left in his hand.) Anything on it? (LEROY looks at it and then looks back at her.) I'd be so glad if you'd read it to me. (LEROY considers her. Possibly she is not putting him on. He looks at the paper. Then he sits and concentrates on it. She comes closer and sits a little downstage of LEROY.)

LEROY (testing). Read this to you?

DORIS (smiling, remembering). Think of it as a concentration exercise, all right? (LEROY regards her for a moment. She smiles back encouragingly. He decides he can trust her. With great difficulty, he starts reading the words on the bit of paper. He speaks painfully, following each syllable with the tip of his finger.)

LEROY. "Please . . . read . . . care . . . carefully." (He takes a breath and takes a quick look at DORIS whose encouraging smile doesn't waver.) "Wel . . . come to the wonder . . . ful . . . world of . . . Maytag . . . wash . . . ing . . . ma . . ." (The light starts to dim out on him.) ". . . ma . . . machines."

ACT TWO

Music.

As the houselights dim to black, we hear music. It is music that could have been composed by BRUNO, but may, in fact, have been created by your own talent or selected to suit the circumstance. It is modern, energetic, joyous and, if possible, played on a synthesizer.

As the music continues, a spot of light comes up on BRUNO, seated in a chair DC facing the audience. He is wearing earphones and occasionally reaches forward to make adjustments on an imaginary tape deck. He is within the special world of his own music and what we are hearing is evidently what he is hearing through his earphones.

Bruno's father, ANGELO, and his uncle, MARIO, come into the edge of the light in which we see BRUNO.

MARIO. Bruno . . . (BRUNO doesn't hear him. To ANGELO.) What's he doing?
ANGELO. Spending his life in the basement, hooked up. (Defensively.) There's big money in this kind of music. The stars

44

are the financial elite.

MARIO. So when do you finish paying for the synthesizer?

ANGELO. Three years. (He taps BRUNO on the shoulder.)
Bruno . . . (BRUNO sees MARIO and ANGELO, reaches forward to turn a dial, and the music stops. He takes off his headset.) Mario brought his van and a couple guys to take the
synthesizer back to school.

BRUNO (getting up). Thank you, Uncle Mario.

ANGELO. Sophomore year. (Hopefully.) Maybe you'll have
more fun sophomore year.

MARIO (as he reaches forward, a cassette concealed in his hand,
and apparently takes it out of a recorder). This was what you
were hearing? (As BRUNO nods.) How about *we* hear it?

BRUNO. No time. We better get going, Poppa. First day of the
new term.

MARIO (starting off). Meet you over there.

ANGELO (taking the cassette from MARIO as he passes). My
son's private listening. (He looks at BRUNO, then turns his
chair so it faces L.) Get in the cab. (BRUNO seats himself in
the chair as ANGELO turns an adjoining chair in the same
direction. He speaks as he does this.) You spent your entire
vacation in the basement with the private music. It's not
natural. You never go out with a pretty girl. (Traffic noises
come up as ANGELO drives.)

BRUNO (embarrassed). Get off my case, will ya, Poppa?

ANGELO. When I was your age —

BRUNO. Please!

ANGELO. I had girlfriends. I had lots of girlfriends.

BRUNO. I got music.

ANGELO. For what? For yourself? For your headset? Do I
hear it anymore? Does your mama hear it? Do your friends
hear it? Do you have any friends?

BRUNO. I told you, I don't have the time.

ANGELO. You told me. But it's not natural. When I was your age —

BRUNO (exploding). You're not my age. Nobody's my age. Maybe I'm ahead of my time. (This is his real fear.) Maybe . . . maybe I don't think people will like my stuff.

ANGELO (angrily honking an imaginary horn at someone). How do you know what people will like? How do they know if they don't hear it? How do they hear it if you don't play it for them? (He honks again.) How do they recognize talent . . . and give scholarships . . . contracts . . . awards?

BRUNO. Maybe they don't. Maybe I die undiscovered. Maybe my ghost gets the Grammys.

ANGELO. Maybe! Maybe! Maybe!

BRUNO (trying to cut ANGELO short). Forty-sixth street . . . (As ANGELO brings the imaginary taxi to a screeching stop.)

ANGELO. Did I build a studio in the basement for a ghost? Did I spend seven thousand dollars on equipment for a ghost? (Light comes up.)

BRUNO. Please . . .

ANGELO (waving the cassette at BRUNO). Does your mama cook and clean and wear old clothes for a ghost?

(STUDENTS ready for the start of school enter R and L. They are loaded down with paraphenalia and ad lib as they enter.)

BRUNO (as the STUDENTS enter, dying of embarrassment). They'll hear you! (He starts off quickly.) I have to go to homeroom!

ANGELO (shouting after BRUNO). *Elton John's mother has six mink coats!*

(LEROY, carrying his huge portable stereo, enters and almost bumps into MRS. SHERWOOD, entering from another direction.)

LEROY. Thought you retired.

MRS. SHERWOOD (pointedly). Too much unfinished business, Mr. Johnson. (She points at the stereo.) And don't bring that into my classroom. (As she hurries off, LEROY makes a gesture after her. ANGELO comes up to LEROY, still holding the cassette.)

ANGELO. Could I ask you something? I'm Bruno Martelli's father.

(As ANGELO and LEROY go into a private conversation, MONTGOMERY comes on L, calling across to DORIS coming on R.)

MONTGOMERY. Doris!

(DORIS lights up as she sees MONTGOMERY, but she's closely followed by MRS. SCHWARTZ.)

MONTGOMERY (delighted). You're right on time.

MRS. SCHWARTZ. You think we'd be late? Never!

MONTGOMERY (to DORIS). You didn't forget your promise? First day of school, we have dinner and see a show. I have tickets for —

MRS. SCHWARTZ. She can't. She's singing tonight for a birthday party at the Silburmanns'.

DORIS. I promised Montgomery.

MRS. SCHWARTZ. I promised the Silburmanns. (To MONTGOMERY.) Sorry. (To DORIS.) I ironed your pink dress with the pink ribbons.

DORIS. I *hate* the pink dress! I *hate* the pink ribbons! I *hate* the —

MRS. SCHWARTZ (defensively). It's an exposure . . . a chance to sing.

DORIS. *Happy Birthday* to three-year-olds?

MONTGOMERY (helping DORIS). Another night, Doris. (DORIS clenches both fists with frustration.)

(NICOLE and JOY cross downstage.)

NICOLE. I've got to lose fifteen pounds.

JOY. It always comes off my bust — which doesn't help.

NICOLE. I don't care where it comes off.

(RALPH makes a big entrance.)

MRS. SCHWARTZ (jostling Doris' arm). Doris . . .

RALPH. Ring the bells! I'm back! Now you can start the school!

MRS. SCHWARTZ (to DORIS). We don't want to be late.

DORIS. We're early. (She calls to RALPH.) Where were you all summer?

RALPH. (Big deal. He heads off.) Looking after my two chicks.

DORIS (calling after RALPH). Ralph . . . (At this, everything is cut off short by an explosion of music. ALL look over to where ANGELO has put Leroy's huge portable stereo on one of the chairs, inserted the cassette, and turned it on loud. *Note: The portable may be the actual sound source or just the apparent source as the music is either live or played over the theater loudspeakers.*)

ANGELO (responding to their stares with a proclamation). My

son's music.

LEROY. (He knows.) We heard it before! (If appropriate.)
Lyrics, too.

ANGELO (eagerly). He plays it for you sometimes?

COCO (dancing over to the music). He forgets to turn off the
speaker sometimes.

PHENICIA (to ANGELO). Louder, man.

LEROY (making dance moves to the music, loving it). All right!

ANGELO (anxious to believe this). All right?

LEROY (shouting over the increased volume). *All right*! (He
and COCO lead the dance with other STUDENTS coming into
it and each, in some personal way, joining the joy and dynamics
of this music. *If there are lyrics, the STUDENTS can sing
them. After all, they've overheard BRUNO rehearsing. The
entire "student" cast participates in this musical opening for
the second act which may be a small, improvised appreciation
of this special music or as big and as energetic a production
number as you care to make it*.)

ANGELO (shouting proudly, during the above). My son . . .
Bruno Martelli! *Bruno Martelli wrote the music*!

(At this, the only non-participant, BRUNO, rushes onstage, a-
ghast at what is happening.)

BRUNO. Poppa!

ANGELO (ignoring BRUNO, shouting to the world). Today
Forty-sixth Street! Tomorrow Madison Square Garden!

BRUNO (frantically). *Poppa*!

COCO (dancing past BRUNO). Sounds good! (There is growing
pandemonium with the STUDENTS totally involved in the
musical experience.)

BRUNO (shouting into Angelo's ear). You had no right to take
my tape. It wasn't ready.

ANGELO (slapping Bruno's back). Take a look at the people! (He roars.) They don't know it isn't ready! They like it. (He turns it even louder as BRUNO, dumbfounded, turns to look for himself. *It's true! They like it!* The music concludes and the STUDENTS freeze in their final positions. In the moment of silence, the school bell rings. Back to real life. They move off into school, talking quietly to each other as they go. ANGELO takes out the cassette, hands the stereo back to LEROY, then speaks quietly.) Hope I didn't wear out your batteries.

LEROY (heading off to class, with a smile). I got lotsa batteries.

ANGELO (handing the cassette back to BRUNO, hopefully). Maybe you're gonna get lotsa friends . . . (BRUNO doesn't know what to say. He takes the cassette and runs off into school. ANGELO takes a deep and joyous breath. He lets it out with gusto and goes off. There is an instant of quiet.)

(MRS. SHERWOOD comes on R.)

MRS. SHERWOOD. First thing this morning, I fixed a special breakfast for my husband who isn't all that well. Then I came here to . . . (She hesitates as she sees LEROY crossing to his chair desk.) . . . to deal with my unfinished business. (Half angry.) It isn't enough to be street smart. It isn't enough to be fluent in ghetto. (Frustrated.) The Board of Education expects every graduate to be able to read, write and speak standard English. They expect me to get through that granite boulder some of them put between us . . . compounded of "I won't!" and "I can't!"

(HILARY VAN DOREN, an elegant young ballerina, crosses to her chair desk.)

MRS. SHERWOOD. We get a variety at Performing Arts. This new student was driven to school in a white limousine. (As other STUDENTS take their place in class, she suddenly remembers.) The word for today.

(As MRS. SHERWOOD crosses to her desk, DORIS enters with MONTGOMERY.)

DORIS. All Ralph Garcy wants is a laugh. He doesn't take anything seriously.

MONTGOMERY. He *is* funny.

DORIS. I don't know how he got into the school. He just makes jokes and goofs off.

MONTGOMERY (as he seats himself). Probably covering up a lot of pain.

DORIS (also sitting). Ralph Garcy?

MONTGOMERY (quietly). Everyone is covering up a lot of pain.

LEROY (greeting DORIS). Hey, Doris . . .

DORIS (back to him, right on). Washing machine! (As LEROY laughs, MRS. SHERWOOD raps for order.)

MRS. SHERWOOD. I want this room quiet. I'm not speaking until I hear silence.

(RALPH hurries in and goes to his chair.)

RALPH (in a Donald Duck voice). Silence!

MRS. SHERWOOD. We have a new student joining our homeroom this year. Her name is Hilary Van Doren. She's a ballet major in the Dance Department. I know you'll make her feel at home.

RALPH (to HILARY). Your place or mine?

MRS. SHERWOOD. The word for today is "pretension" . . . an

allegation of doubtful value . . . a claim or right to attention . . . or honor because of merit, aspiration, or intention. Pretentiousness . . . vanity. (She looks about.) Who wants to use it in a sentence?

COCO (raising her hand). Coming to school in a white limousine . . . like some people . . . is displaying pretension.

MRS. SHERWOOD. Aside from a gratuitous clause, the use of the word is essentially correct. Who has another example? (As HILARY raises her hand.) Yes. Hilary.

HILARY (calmly). Coming to school at all . . . for some people . . . is displaying pretension. (The STUDENTS laugh. COCO is burned.)

(At the other side of the stage, MISS BERG and LYDIA lead DANCE STUDENTS into warm-up exercises.)

MRS. SHERWOOD (amused). I think we've got a handle on pretension. (The lights dim on the classroom area and come up on the dance class area. With this, we hear some music that accompanies the exercises. As the lighting shifts.) Your assignment for tomorrow . . . including you, Mr. Johnson . . . is to read the short story by Robert Louis Stevenson, *The Sire de Maletroit's Door*. (STUDENTS cross from the classroom area to join the OTHERS in the dance area as MRS. SHERWOOD exits L.)

MARIANNE (to HILARY). I love your outfit.

HILARY. My wicked stepmother bought it for me.

MARIANNE. I wouldn't mind that kind of wicked.

HILARY. She didn't do it for me. She wants my father to think she cares. Besides, she loves shopping. (As she spins across the stage.) It turns her on . . . and on . . . and on . . .

PHENICIA (to LEROY, as they cross). Muhammad Anderson is giving a talk tonight on African consciousness. Right after Swahili class.

LEROY. Sorry, baby.

PHENICIA (following LEROY). Tomorrow there's a slide show on The Uganda Experience . . .

LEROY. I'm booked. What are you? A walking bulletin board? (ALL begin to go into their exercises.)

MISS BERG (coming up to LISA). Where's the sweat, Lisa?

LISA (defensively). I'm working on it.

MISS BERG. You're not working hard enough.

LISA. No matter how much I —

MISS BERG. Less lip; more sweat. (HILARY leads LISA into a deep forward bend at the bottom of which LISA half whispers.)

LISA. It doesn't help when the head of the Dance Department hates you.

MISS BERG (hearing the remark anyway). When I say extensions, Lisa, I don't mean your mouth. (LEROY is amused at this, then stops cold as he sees MISS BERG staring at him. She indicates his cut-offs.) I told you —

LEROY. I got 'em. I just forgot 'em.

HILARY (to LISA). What's he talking about?

LISA. Tights. He won't wear 'em. Gets in the way of his image.

HILARY. If he expects to dance ballet . . .

LYDIA (to LEROY, amused). Gymnasts wear tights. Football players wear tights . . .

MISS BERG (to LEROY). Tomorrow. (She gestures R. Generally.) Let's move it over to the barre and get to some real work. (ALL groan as they start off R.)

LEROY (softly defiant). But Leroy . . . he *ain't* wearin' tights.

HILARY. C'est dommage.

LYDIA. What's that?

HILARY (slightly condescending). That's French, my dear. (She and LYDIA cross R.)

LYDIA (frankly). What are you doing at Performing Arts? You could —

HILARY. I want to make it here . . . then no one can say I bought in with my father's money.

LYDIA (curiously). *Why* do you want to make it at all?

HILARY (talking down to LYDIA). I don't think you'd really be able to dig my jive.

LYDIA (stopping, facing HILARY, sweetly). Let me try. You want to dance all the classic roles before you're twenty-one. You want *Giselles* and *Coppelias* coming out of your feet . . . and sleeping beauties . . . and the swan. You want bravos in Stuttgart and Leningrad and Monte Carlo! Then you'll dance a special New Year's Eve performance of *Gâitè Parisienne* at the Met! (As HILARY is half stunned. Gently.) Something like that?

HILARY (nodding, swallowing). Something like that.

LYDIA (echoing MISS BERG). Then let's move it over to the barre and get to some real work.

(As the subdued HILARY follows LYDIA off R, the light comes up at L where a seated semi-circle is forming around MR. FARRELL as he continues a lecture.)

MR. FARRELL. Last year we concentrated on simple observation . . . observing yourself doing everyday things . . . developing an accute sense memory . . . noticing the way you deal with the physical world. Isolating particular details. (To his point.) This year we'll turn that observation inward

and work on recreating emotional states . . . joy, sorrow, fear,
anger. It'll be harder because you'll have to expose a little more
of yourself.

RALPH (jumping up and exposing himself by opening his jacket
in the direction of his favorite target). Doris! Wow!

MR. FARRELL. Sit down. (He continues.) For some of you,
exposing something of yourself won't be too difficult. For
others . . . (He looks directly at RALPH.) . . . for others it
may be impossible. (The lights begin to dim on this area.)
Now . . . for your first exercise, I want you to start thinking
of a painful moment. I want you to recreate a difficult
memory; a painful moment in which you first realized something important about yourself.

(The bell rings. STUDENTS get up and cross R as OTHERS
come in R and cross L. DORIS crosses downstage with
MONTGOMERY.)

DORIS (to MONTGOMERY). What painful memory? I know
I must have them but I don't know if I can find one.

MONTGOMERY (cheerfully). I have lots. You can borrow one
of mine.

DORIS. Such as?

MONTGOMERY. Such as . . . I used to wet my bed. You can
have that one. (Helpfully.) It's painful.

DORIS. No thank you.

MONTGOMERY. Then there was the last time my father packed
his bags and left us. Or the first time my mother took the red-
eye to Los Angeles and didn't come back for six weeks.

DORIS. Those don't really help . . .

(MRS. SHERWOOD enters carrying some books and crosses L to R.)

MONTGOMERY. In that case, I'll tell you my special . . .

DORIS. Your special? (She is hesitant.) You want to talk about it?

MONTGOMERY. Maybe it's time. (He gestures for DORIS to go on ahead.) You won't want to miss this one.

(LEROY, on roller skates, enters DR as MONTGOMERY and DORIS exit UR.)

MRS. SHERWOOD. Leroy!

LEROY (skidding to a halt). Yes, ma'am?

MRS. SHERWOOD. What are you wearing?

LEROY (innocently reaching up and pulling something off his head). A hat?

MRS. SHERWOOD. On your feet.

LEROY (with elaborate surprise). Oh, those. Yeah, well, they help me get around so's I can fly from class to class quicker. Helps me get more learning in.

MRS. SHERWOOD. What about your book report?

LEROY. I done it.

MRS. SHERWOOD. You *did* it.

LEROY. Yeah.

MRS. SHERWOOD. *The Best of Playboy* is not Robert Louis

Stevenson. And it's certainly not a book report.

LEROY. It's readin', ain't it?

MRS. SHERWOOD (looking at her books). So are *Catcher in the Rye, Crime and Punishment, The Brothers Karamazov, Great Expectations.* You've heard of them?

LEROY. I may've caught a couple on t.v.

MRS. SHERWOOD (a sudden plea). If you don't read, you're missing so much.

LEROY (outraged at what he perceives as injustice). You ain't seen improvement? You ain't seen —

MRS. SHERWOOD (the words bursting out of her). I want more! I want much more!

LEROY. You don't get more! You don't get nuthin'! You don't —

MRS. SHERWOOD (stopping LEROY by shoving a book into his hand). Read this. *Othello.* About a black nobleman. A thousand words. Two weeks.

LEROY. Or what?

MRS. SHERWOOD (emphatically). Or you'll be skating right out of the school, Mr. Johnson. (LEROY angrily skates away. As MRS. SHERWOOD turns and goes off R, he makes a gesture after her, then quickly skates off L.)

(As the action between MRS. SHERWOOD and LEROY takes place, MR. SHOROFSKY comes on R with sheet music in his hands. At the same time, some MUSIC STUDENTS come on carrying instruments. They ad lib as they take their places. *It is possible to use student musicians as extras here.* BRUNO also enters, DR and downstage of this, pursued by COCO.)

COCO (to BRUNO). I'm talking about getting up a band.

BRUNO. I don't like bands. They crowd me. I prefer my basement . . . no people.

COCO. Hey, there's a lot of money out there. Tea dances and parties. Weddings and bar mitzvahs . . .

BRUNO. I don't want the hassle.

COCO (no problem). I'll take care of everything. Bookings. Travel arrangements. Costume designs.

BRUNO. What costume designs?

COCO. Sequins and stuff, and a see-through something for me or maybe low-cut. Your music is wicked, but . . . (She poses.) . . . we gotta give 'em visuals . . . Visuals book bands. (Asked as he hesitates. Challenging.) What's the matter, Bruno? You not up to it?

MR. SHOROFSKY (calling to BRUNO, irritated). Whenever you're ready, Mr. Martelli.

BRUNO. Coming. (He eyes Coco's youthful, undeveloped chest.) I just don't think our visuals are up to it. (As he hurries over to take his place, the startled COCO looks after him. Then, shaking her head and laughing to herself, she exits R.)

MR. SHOROFSKY (as BRUNO gets to his chair). We're waiting. Mozart is waiting. (BRUNO picks up a violin and grabs the bow.) That's a violin bow, Mr. Martelli . . . not a baseball bat. Hold it with respect.

BRUNO (doubtfully, as he considers the bow). Respect?

MR. SHOROFSKY (nodding). And join us in playing *Eine Kleine Nachtmusik* . . . as Mozart would like it.

BRUNO (in spite of himself). No.

MR. SHOROFSKY (startled). What?

BRUNO. Mozart wouldn't do it this way. (He answers Shorofsky's bewilderment.) Not today. Not now.

MR. SHOROFSKY. Do what?

BRUNO. This bowing business. He'd just plug his keyboard into a socket, play with his oscillators, and have string quartets coming out of his fingers. And symphonies . . .

MR. SHOROFSKY. And who would play these science fiction symphonies?

BRUNO. He would.

MR. SHOROFSKY. By himself?

BRUNO. He'd overdub and mix. Of course he couldn't make the same old noise exactly.

MR. SHOROFSKY. The same old noise?

BRUNO. He'd sound electric. He'd have spacier strings and horns and —

MR. SHORFOSKY. One man is not an orchestra.

BRUNO. Who needs orchestras?

MR. SHOROFSKY. I do. (He considers BRUNO.) But what is it you need? Tell me *your* vision.

BRUNO (collecting himself, making a serious reply). One human being . . . and electronic equipment . . . the single version of one pair of hands, one mind creating . . . music.

MR. SHOROFSKY (equally serious). I respect that, Mr. Martelli, as I ask your respect and participation here in my vision . . . music that is a harmonious blend of a group of instruments playing in concert, each musician making an individual contribution to the melodious whole. (He taps on the podium with his baton.) Class . . . (To BRUNO.) . . . Your violin and your bow, Mr. Martelli.

BRUNO (serious but smiling). With respect, Mr. Shorofsky. (As the lights dim on the music class, MR. SHOROFSKY brings down his baton to start the music which may be live or mimed to a recording.)

(Light comes up DL revealing DORIS and MONTGOMERY who are listening to the softly played music.)

DORIS. The music is so organized . . . makes me want to get

my act together.

MONTGOMERY. *A Little Night Music* . . . the perfect choice . . . that's what we are.

DORIS. When you told me your special pain, I started wondering . . . why I wasn't more surprised. Did I guess something about it?

MONTGOMERY. Maybe. You're my friend.

DORIS. After you told me, I looked around. The world was still the same. The sky was still blue. The street was still dirty. (She turns to MONTGOMERY, deeply concerned.) But don't tell that memory in class.

MONTGOMERY. It's the most painful.

DORIS. Mr. Farrell didn't say "the most painful." He just said "painful."

MONTGOMERY. We're supposed to expose ourselves.

DORIS. Think what Ralph Garcy would say.

(The music ends and the MUSIC STUDENTS go off R as the DRAMA STUDENTS enter L to form around MR. FARRELL.)

MONTGOMERY (smiling). A pie in the face comes with the job. That's what my mom says and she should know.

DORIS. But don't ask for it.

MONTGOMERY. We're performers. We're not supposed to be afraid of what people might say about us.

MR. FARRELL (calling). Montgomery . . . We'll have you go first. (MONTGOMERY crosses to sit in a separate wooden chair that has been placed so that he faces the class, but he is turned partly away from the audience. DORIS, still in the pool of light DL, speaks out to the audience.)

DORIS. He was alone in that chair, speaking softly. There was silence as he spoke except for a few embarrassed coughs. He spoke without apparent emotion. He didn't whine or make verbal plays for pity . . . just speaking in a quiet, level voice . . . yet everyone sensed some of the pain at which he was just hinting . . . (She looks back to MONTGOMERY, then front again.) A lonely child, a famous mother who spent most of her time away. A father who'd rejected him . . . and then a medical problem. (MONTGOMERY shifts his chair so that the audience can see him now, and he picks up on the recital himself.)

MONTGOMERY. I was too young to understand the problem . . . too young to know what was happening. I had a growth . . . a tumor . . . in an awkward place . . . an embarrassing place.

RALPH (guessing correctly, in a high pitch). Eeep!

MR. FARRELL (quietly emphatic). Shut up, Ralph.

MONTGOMERY (nodding agreement with RALPH). A place about which to make jokes . . . but I was still too young to get it. Later I started realizing that there was something not happening about me. People kept saying, "you'll grow out of it." But I did not grow out of it and finally Dr. Goldin leveled with me. In that moment, I found out that it wouldn't make sense for me to get married and that I would never be a father. (He smiles.) There's a line in a song by Alan Jay Lerner. It goes . . . "There's more to us than surgeons can remove." I hold onto that and I want to make it true. (He tries to lighten up.) It doesn't bother me that much anymore. I have friends. I'm pretty well adjusted. Really. I mean, that doesn't make me queer or anything. I just like people who like me. (ALL are hushed as he finishes.)

MR. FARRELL (after a moment). Thank you, Montgomery. Now, who's next? I guess that's Doris. (DORIS comes into the scene, still talking to the audience as she crosses to the chair just vacated by MONTGOMERY. At the point when she sits down, she is then speaking to the other STUDENTS.)

DORIS. My painful moment, like my life, seems trivial. I was dressed up like an overgrown Shirley Temple in that pink dress with the pink ribbons . . . and I was singing *Happy Birthday To You* to a pampered, coddled three-year-old in a paper hat who sat squirming and crying at the head of a table with fourteen other three-year-olds all making one horrible racket . . . while my mother gets out her instamatic camera to immortalize that miserable occasion. (Angrily.) Barbra Streisand could never have gone through all this. This was humiliation . . . this was pain . . . this was . . . this was . . . (She smiles.) . . . my assignment, Mr. Farrell.

MR. FARRELL. Thank you, Doris. Now . . . what did you realize about yourself? (DORIS takes a breath as she considers.)

DORIS. I didn't belong there. I don't like birthday parties. Or pink dresses. Or the Silburmanns. Or Brooklyn. Or even . . . being Jewish. I mean, it's not bad, but it's not all I am.

MR. FARRELL. Who are you?

DORIS. I don't *know* who I am. (Realizing.) And I never will if I just do what other people want me to do and wear what they want me to wear and sing what they want me to sing. (A cry.) I'm not a dressed-up parakeet! (She takes another breath.) I'm sixteen. I have to assert *myself* . . . *myself* . . . sometime.

MR. FARRELL (gently, as DORIS pauses). Okay, Doris. (He turns.) Ralph . . . you're next.

RALPH. All right . . . (He goes over to the chair and pulls DORIS up out of it.) Make way . . . star time.

DORIS (making way). Your throne . . . Sir Laurence. (RALPH

seats himself as DORIS joins the semi-circle. He takes a breath, some of the pizazz draining away. He looks a bit small and thin and alone. Without looking at MR. FARRELL or at any of the other STUDENTS, he begins to talk.)

RALPH. I came home from school, you know, like always. I'm late because I got one or two little pieces of business, and it's January and Santa Claus has just ripped everybody off and split for Igloo City. I switch on the t.v. and some dude is sayin' that Freddie Prinze put this gun in his mouth, makin' noise like he meant to kill himself. And everybody knows it was an accident. (He turns to talk directly to the other STUDENTS.) He was jokin', you know. He was always jokin'. You had to laugh. Sometimes you didn't even *want* to laugh. And you laughed anyway. Like it was a gift he had. All you had to do was look into that man's eyes to know he wasn't into death. The world had to get him . . . because he didn't think livin' was such a heavy trip. They had to say he was depressed and suicidal . . . 'cause the world gotta take itself real serious. We can't have happy people walkin' around this planet. I don't pay. (Angrily.) No, there's gotta be something *wrong* with us . . . so that the plastic surgeons and the witch doctors and the underarm deodorant people can stay in business . . . (He breaks off, unable to continue.)

MR. FARRELL (after a brief pause). Does all this make you realize something about yourself?

RALPH. What?

MR. FARRELL. How does it affect you?

RALPH (bitterly). I'm here. In this school. Getting back at it. For Freddie.

MR. FARRELL. Take it easy, Ralph. (Sympathetically.) You

want them laughing with you, not at you. (The school bell rings.)

RALPH. I want 'em laughing, *period*!

MR. FARRELL. Tomorrow I want to hear Joy, Marianne and Deirdre. (To MONTGOMERY.) Montgomery, I want you to direct a scene . . . prepare it for class. Next Friday. (He considers.) Paddy Cheyevsky's *Marty*. The lonely schoolteacher can be Doris.

MONTGOMERY. And Marty?

MR. FARRELL. The gentle, shy, lonely middle-aged man . . . we'll try Ralph. (As RALPH is startled.) A chance to stretch. (They go off, leaving MONTGOMERY, DORIS and RALPH downstage.)

RALPH. Director, there's one thing I want you to teach this gentle, shy, lonely old man . . . teach him how to sing soprano.

DORIS (to MONTGOMERY). There. I told you so.

RALPH. Hey, that's just a joke, you know. It just came out.

MONTGOMERY. Like me.

RALPH. Yeah. (An uncomfortable pause.) Look, who cares. It's your case. Forget it.

MONTGOMERY. Do you want to rehearse tonight?

RALPH. Tonight I'll be at Catch A Rising Star.

DORIS. You're going on?

RALPH. Looks like.

MONTGOMERY. We'll show up, too. Always bring a claque. We can rehearse later.

RALPH. Maybe. (As DORIS and MONTGOMERY are about to go.) Doris, can I have a word with you in private?

MONTGOMERY (hesitating, then going). See you later.

(Across the stage at R, LISA comes in, sits in a chair, and starts to take off her dance shoes.)

RALPH. I have to tell you something tremendous about Montgomery. (DORIS doesn't trust him, but she's curious.) He's up for a big award . . . a great honor.

DORIS (knowing she'll regret this, but asking anyway). What honor?

RALPH (knocked out by his own wit). The No-Ball Prize for Drama! (DORIS clenches her fists with anger as the laughing RALPH scampers off L. She expels a breath and then goes off L.)

(MISS BERG enters R and approaches LISA.)

MISS BERG. Where are the blisters, Lisa?

LISA (quickly touching her foot, but it's no help). It's my shoes. They protect my feet.

MISS BERG. No shoe stops blisters.

LISA. They're from Capezio. (As MISS BERG is skeptical.) And I've been sick.

MISS BERG. Dancers don't get sick. You're not working hard enough.

LISA. The doctor told me to take it easy for a week or two. Don't you believe me? I brought a note.

MISS BERG. I believe you, but I don't have room for you in this class anymore. There isn't time or space for someone who isn't dedicated.

LISA. I *am* dedicated!

MISS BERG. I'm sorry. I don't see it.

LISA. I got into the school, didn't I?

MISS BERG. We made a mistake. Sometimes it doesn't work out. I'm sorry.

LISA. I don't know what I'll do if I can't dance.

MISS BERG. You'll get over it.

LISA. I'll work harder. I promise. I'll be better.

MISS BERG. Better isn't good enough. I don't think you'll ever be good enough and I'm saving you a lot of pain by saying it now.

LISA. I don't have to be the best. I just want to be a dancer. (As MISS BERG shakes her head.) What do I . . . tell . . . my mother?

MISS BERG (as she goes off). Ask her to give me a call. I'll explain.

(As MISS BERG exits, COCO comes on with MARIANNE, JOY and PHENICIA. COCO looks at the stricken LISA who is stuffing her dance things into a bag and sliding into her street shoes.)

COCO. She came down on you hard? (As LISA nods.) So life comes down hard.

PHENICIA. Reactionary, honky, Fascist.

MARIANNE. And a Virgo. For sure!

JOY (to LISA). We're going to Catch A Rising Star tonight. Why don't you —

LISA (interrupting, bleakly). She kicked me out!

JOY (finishing). Come with us.

COCO (encouragingly). Hey . . .

JOY. I heard some kids from here might go on.

LISA (overwhelmed). I'm not from *here* anymore.

MARIANNE (considering). Not from the *Dance* Department anymore.

LISA. What d'ya mean?

JOY (getting it). She means —

MARIANNE (cutting in). You give acting performances all the time!

LISA (bewildered). Performances?

MARIANNE (melodramatically). I just slipped a disc in my back!

JOY (joining in). The terrible pain in my pelvis . . .

COCO (gasping as she grabs her foot). I mashed my metatarsal.

PHENICIA. I bring a bulletin from Bellevue. The doctors want me to take a three-week vacation.

MARIANNE. You are one hell of an actress. Get it?

JOY. So switch to the Drama Department.

LISA (seeing a hope). The Drama Department . . .

COCO. C'mon — gotta catch the subway.

LISA. I'll do it! (She snatches up her bag and crosses R, shouting off). Miss Berg . . . there's something I wantta give you . . . right where you need them. (She flings her bag off R.) My *Capezios*! (Laughing, the GIRLS race across the stage. As they go off L, the lights dim except for a bright spot that comes up C.)

(There is the sound of loud applause and cheers, perhaps recorded. During this, STUDENTS come on R and L. They carry a few small tables and chairs, setting a restaurant scene. Meanwhile, the glittering MISTRESS OF CEREMONIES comes into the spotlight. She carries what appears to be a wireless mike. She waves to calm the applause, which may be joined by the entering STUDENTS who whistle and cheer.)

MISTRESS OF CEREMONIES (as the sound comes down). I guess you like that performer. (She glances at her notes.) Ralph Garcy! (More whistles and cheers.) Apparently this boy

is all alone and no one here knows him. (Hoots and whistles.)
This is the night the new talent comes out. Some of these kids
have never been on a stage before and some never will be
again . . . But maybe we're lucky tonight . . . Maybe tonight
we're gonna start another career! (More applause and cheers.)
You want more? You want an encore? (The applause rises.
Shouts of "yes" and "more." She calls off.) Ralph Garcy!
(She calls more loudly.) One more time!

(RALPH, on a great high, comes dancing on, dressed for the
  moment. The MISTRESS OF CEREMONIES joins the dance
  and as they come together, she hands the mike to RALPH.)

MISTRESS OF CEREMONIES. You got it . . . (Aside.) But
  keep it short.
RALPH. Thank you . . . Thank you. Like the lady said, this
  boy is all alone and no one here knows him. (As they respond.)
  No, seriously, my friends are here . . . which is nice. Up
  where I live . . . in the South Bronx . . . that's the country
  just north of Harlem and west of Puerto Rico . . . Up there
  you *gotta* have friends! You can't afford to alienate *any* minority groups. Like the cockroaches. They got a good union. Last
  week fifteen thousand of them marched down my block de-
  manding better housing. And the rats. Throw them something
  under the table or they get ugly. Last week they stole a building. But really . . . I love the South Bronx. Everywhere you
  go from there is up. Everyone's got dreams, see. Big dreams.
  You stop your average boy on a South Bronx street, ask him
  what he wants to be when he grows up . . . An *ex*-junkie. Ask
  your average girl . . . A dynamite hooker. People up there
  can't afford empty dreams . . . except my Uncle Ramon.
  He wanted to move to the country and raise chickens. Last
  month he hits a big number and gets his wish. But his chickens

all died. I asked him why. He said, "I don't know. Maybe I planted them too close." (The MISTRESS OF CEREMONIES gives RALPH a warning gesture that he's running too long.) Hey, I gotta go now. But I wanna tell you you're great. My family thanks you, the winos thank you, the narcs, the cockroaches . . . and I thank you. (He runs off to applause and cheers, handing the mike to the MISTRESS OF CEREMONIES as he goes.)

MISTRESS OF CEREMONIES. You caught a rising star tonight. Now eat up . . . and drink up . . .

(As she goes off, light comes up on a wider area showing STUDENTS at a table. They ad lib conversation as recorded music comes up over the cabaret's speakers. RALPH runs back on, getting calls from those at several tables, to which he responds with waves, as he comes to the table CL to sit with DORIS and MONTGOMERY.)

DORIS. You were wonderful.

RALPH (with mock humbleness). Naaaghh . . .

DORIS. Yes. Really. You know you were.

RALPH (still on his high). I wasn't just wonderful. I was the best . . . (To DORIS.) Say it . . . (To MONTGOMERY.) Say it! *Say it*!

MONTGOMERY. You were the best.

RALPH (as DORIS nods). You said it.

MONTGOMERY. With an encore.

RALPH. It's like . . . electricity. You're up there and those faces are starin' at you, and you're leadin' 'em out . . . building up a positive charge . . . and then . . . *bam*! You hit 'em . . . hit 'em with the juice and they explode . . . and that power goes flowin' back and forth! And it's *you*. You are makin' them laugh. That's the meanest high there is. (He leans back. To the ceiling.) *I love it!*

MONTGOMERY. After we celebrate . . . do you still want to rehearse tonight? You and Doris?

RALPH. Maybe later after I check on my chicks. No way I could sleep tonight. (Excitedly.) It's getting close . . . (He answers their questioning looks.) . . . fame.

DORIS. If a little of that ever came my way, I couldn't handle it.

RALPH. Keep an eye on me, baby. I'll teach you. You ride around in a big customized Dorado, white leather, red paint, stereo tape deck, four speakers. Everybody knows your face, and when you want something, they jump.

MONTGOMERY (hopping up, imitating a flunkie). Can I get you something, sir? The key to Fort Knox? The President's daughter? The cover of *Time* magazine?

DORIS (laughing). Ralph . . . you don't want that. *That's* not your fame. That's Freddie Prinze's fame.

RALPH. I want all of it . . . love me . . . laugh when I tell you . . . with flashbulbs going off in my face.

MONTGOMERY (sitting again). I don't know if I'd care for all that . . .

RALPH (dumbfounded). You kidding or what?

(A handsome WAITER approaches them. It's MICHAEL LAMBERT.)

MICHAEL/WAITER. You kids ready to order?

DORIS (half recognizing MICHAEL, but not sure). I . . . uh . . .

MICHAEL/WAITER. Yes?

DORIS. Are you Michael Lambert?

MICHAEL/WAITER. Sure.

DORIS. I thought so . . . (As MICHAEL doesn't respond.) You don't remember?

MICHAEL/WAITER (a little confused). What?

DORIS. I'm Doris Schwartz. Performing Arts.

MICHAEL/WAITER. Oh, yeah, yeah, sure. Around the corner.

DORIS. And you remember Montgomery MacNeill.

MICHAEL/WAITER. Yeah. (He recalls.) I do. I remember your audition. That was not a bad audition.

DORIS. And Ralph Garcy.

MICHAEL/WAITER. The comic. All from P.A. (A memory stirs in him. He remembers. Wryly.) The good old days.

MONTGOMERY (gently). Hard to appreciate them while they're happening.

DORIS. How was Hollywood?

MICHAEL/WAITER (uncomfortably). Slow. I met some people. I went to some parties. I did a pilot for a series.

DORIS. I didn't see it.

MICHAEL/WAITER (bitterly). Nobody saw it.

DORIS. I'm sorry.

MICHAEL/WAITER. I played a male nurse for two days. On a soap. (He pauses.) I didn't like L.A.

DORIS. Are you studying?

MICHAEL/WAITER (uneasily, embarrassed). I catch a class here and there. I read for a showcase. I got a big call-back coming up next week. (He takes a breath.) Well, what are you kids having? We got a special tonight on fried clams.

DORIS. Uh . . . clams sound good.

RALPH. I'm not staying . . .

MONTGOMERY. I'll have the clams, too. (MICHAEL, eager to escape, goes off with the order.)

DORIS (stunned). Michael Lambert!

RALPH. Who needs him? Look . . . I'll try to see you later.

MONTGOMERY. My apartment. The Palace Theatre building . . .

RALPH. Gotcha . . . (The lights dim out as he hurries off R and the music level comes up. In this moment, the STUDENTS take off the tables and chairs as the lights go to black. In the darkness, a match is struck by MONTGOMERY who lights a candle with it. As this happens, the music goes off. DORIS and MONTGOMERY are seen in the candlelight as they go DCL and sit on two floor cushions while a little supporting light comes up on them.)

DORIS. I like your apartment, but what happened to the furniture?

MONTGOMERY (smiling). It closed in Cincinnati.

DORIS. What closed?

MONTGOMERY. The play my mother thought was going to give her the money to fix up this place.

DORIS (bothered). What happened with Michael Lambert? He was the handsomest . . . the best . . . If Michael Lambert . . . He got "Best Actor" at graduation. William Morris signed him. If *he* couldn't make it, how can I?

MONTGOMERY. Hey, come on!

DORIS. I'm serious.

MONTGOMERY. All my life I've seen guys like Michael Lambert come and go.

DORIS. Are you serious?

MONTGOMERY. There was a Michael Lambert in almost every one of my mother's plays. A young guy who could act a little and look impressive. They're called juveniles.

DORIS. That's not fair.

MONTGOMERY. If you have a nickel, you could buy six of them.

DORIS (insisting). They're stars.

MONTGOMERY. They're candles. They don't give off a lot of light . . . like this baby. Pretty, right? But you can't work by it and you can't read by it. (He holds the candle up high.) This has nothing to do with you or me . . . or with Ralph. We're not pretty people. We have something better going for us.

(RALPH walks into the scene as more light comes up.)

RALPH (calling ahead to DORIS and MONTGOMERY). Speak for yourself. I'm pretty people.

DORIS (pleased). You came . . .

RALPH. It's my right. (To MONTGOMERY.) All this your apartment? (MONTGOMERY nods and blows out the candle.) Ay, Maria! Fifteen Puerto Rican families with all their furniture could fit in here and still have room to take in boarders! (Curiously.) So what do we have better going for us?

MONTGOMERY. Michael Lambert had it too easy. We've all had a little pain.

RALPH (are-you-out-of-your-mind). Pain?

MONTGOMERY. Makes you a little stronger . . . to deal with rejection; to deal with success!

RALPH (as if it's all nonsense). You don't deal with success. You open champagne . . .

DORIS (concerned). Are you here to rehearse or give out autographs?

RALPH (opening his arms to DORIS). Ready for the scene in the dance hall?

MONTGOMERY (as DORIS hesitates). Let's create a little atmosphere. (As he reaches forward to turn on an imaginary tape deck.) This is where Marty meets the lovely schoolteacher . . . (Old-fashioned dance music comes up.) I'm going to add a little effect. (MONTGOMERY picks up a small, mirrored

globe, and a flashlight from beside his cushion. RALPH continues to hold out his arms to DORIS.)

RALPH. You gonna do the scene or not?

DORIS (still hesitating). Of course.

RALPH. We have to dance. It's a period piece. Touch dancing.

DORIS. I'll be awkward.

MONTGOMERY.   Awkward works for the scene. (Spinning
spots of light reflect off the turning globe that MONTGOMERY
holds in one hand, illuminated by the flashlight he holds in his
other hand. Along with the music, the lights create a sense of
the old Roseland Dance Hall. DORIS moves into Ralph's arms
and they move in a slow circle) Your line, Ralph.

RALPH (in the role). "You get knocked around long enough,
you get to be a real professor of pain. I know exactly how you
feel. And I also want you to know I'm having a very good time
with you now and I'm really enjoying myself. So you see,
you're not such a dog as you think you are."

DORIS (smiling up to RALPH, in character). "I'm having a very
good time, too!"

RALPH (as Marty).   "So, I guess I'm not such a dog as I think
I am."

DORIS.   "You're a very nice guy and I don't know why some
girl hasn't grabbed you off long ago."

RALPH.   "I don't know either." (He gives DORIS a small kiss.)
"I think I'm a very nice guy." (DORIS nods in reply, and he
kisses her again.) "I also think I'm a pretty smart guy . . . in
my own way."

DORIS.   "I think you are . . ." (Impulsively, she kisses RALPH,
and then they kiss again — which is not part of the script as
MONTGOMERY points out.)

MONTGOMERY. Wait. You shouldn't kiss here. (Ignoring him,
DORIS and RALPH kiss again.)   There's a whole speech
yet . . .   (RALPH and DORIS have gone into another world.

The lights dim to black.) This isn't where . . . (Recognizing
that DORIS and RALPH are no longer with him, he reaches
forward to turn up the music and then again shines his flashlight on the spinning globe as the circling spots of light become
the only illumination of the couple. MONTGOMERY feels
alone and empty. A cry.) Damn it! (He snaps off the flashlight and the music cuts out.)

(A spot of light comes up DL, revealing MRS. SHERWOOD.)

MRS. SHERWOOD. The semesters start going by faster and
faster like a speeded-up clock. First they're auditioning for
the freshman class . . . Then they're planning the senior
class show. My husband's condition keeps getting worse and
I've had to start thinking about early retirement . . . so I can
be with him.

(Meanwhile, light comes up as STUDENTS enter for the start of
still another term. BRUNO comes in, leafing through sheet
music.)

BRUNO (calling back off). Thanks for the lift, Poppa.

(As BRUNO goes into the classroom area, LEROY enters, followed by PHENICIA who is trying to get his attention.)

PHENICIA. Leroy, it's about slavery. A folk ballet based on the
exploitation of black people in the deep down home.
LEROY. Sorry, sugar. I'm gonna work on a modern thing with
Lydia and Miss Berg. And my afternoons are very busy.
MRS. SHERWOOD (as she watches LEROY go, ruefully). Not
with homework.

(Other STUDENTS enter and cross to the classroom area.)

MRS. SHERWOOD. Their lives have to be changing, but maybe I'm so burnt out, I can't see it. (She starts off L.) I need the perfect new word to start this new term.

(DORIS enters R, only to be stopped by MRS. SCHWARTZ, who takes hold of her arm.)

DORIS. I told you. I'm going to change my name.
MRS. SCHWARTZ. I'll call you Doris like I always have.
DORIS. I won't answer.
MRS. SCHWARTZ. Barbra Streisand didn't change her name.
DORIS. Barbra Streisand didn't have a name like Doris Schwartz.
MRS. SCHWARTZ. It's a perfectly good name.
DORIS. For a perfectly good person. A dumpy, boring, non-descript, perfectly good person.

(RALPH crosses on, waving briefly to DORIS as he passes.)

MRS. SCHWARTZ (suspiciously). Does this come from staying out late all those nights?
DORIS (looking after RALPH). No late nights in quite a while.
MRS. SCHWARTZ. I have a lot of friends named Doris.
DORIS. I don't want a middle-aged name. From now on, call me Dominique.
MRS. SCHWARTZ. That's ridiculous.
DORIS. It's French.
MRS. SCHWARTZ. It isn't you.
DORIS. I'll grow into it.
MRS. SCHWARTZ. Dominique Schwartz?
DORIS. Dominique Dupont. (As MRS. SCHWARTZ continues,

STUDENTS take their places in Mrs. Sherwood's classroom.)

MRS. SCHWARTZ (bewildered). Where did my Doris go?

DORIS (going to class). I'm trying to find out. (MRS. SHER-
WOOD enters the classroom area. MRS. SCHWARTZ exits
R.)

MRS. SHERWOOD. The word for today is "metamorphosis."
A change of physical form, structure or substance . . . a
striking alteration in appearance, character or circumstance.

LISA (raising her hand). A caterpillar undergoes a metamorphosis when it becomes a butterfly.

MRS. SHERWOOD. All right. Coco?

COCO (looking at HILARY). For some people . . . getting a
nose job is a metamorphosis.

HILARY. All the better to smell you with, my dear.

MRS. SHERWOOD (reprimanding). Hilary . . .

DORIS (regarding HILARY with a touch of envy). My guess
is . . . you were born beautiful.

HILARY (slightly surprised, answering seriously). My mother
once told me . . . beautiful isn't something you're born.
It's something you practice.

MRS. SHERWOOD (back to her word). Ralph . . . (RALPH is
slouched in his chair, only half awake.) Ralph!

RALPH (looking at MRS. SHERWOOD with one eye). Time to
get up?

MRS. SHERWOOD. The new word. Metamorphosis.

RALPH (with an effort). Okay . . . I met a morphosis on the
street. (The STUDENTS groan. DORIS is disappointed. The
bell rings.)

MRS. SHERWOOD. Your assignment for tomorrow . . . the
first three chapters of Ray Bradbury's *Dandelion Wine*.

RALPH. I'll drink to that . . .

LEROY. *Three* chapters!

MRS. SHERWOOD. You got the message, Mr. Johnson?

LEROY (as he goes). I got the message on day one, dragon-face. (MRS. SHERWOOD winces at his attitude as she goes off. DORIS, RALPH and MONTGOMERY go DC.)

RALPH (to MONTGOMERY). I need something.

DORIS. Sleep.

RALPH. Something to get me flying again.

MONTGOMERY. Looks like you've already flown.

RALPH. Don't work my case.

DORIS. We never see you anymore.

RALPH. You see me plenty.

DORIS. Asleep in class.

RALPH. I'm out most of the night with the people who count. I'm working on the future.

DORIS. Because Freddie did it. And that's how he died. He could have been a real actor.

RALPH. He *was* a real actor.

DORIS. He told jokes. But that's not enough. Not for you.

RALPH. Stop it!

DORIS. I won't stop. You're an original. The original Ralph Garcy. You don't have to be someone else.

RALPH. Thanks a lot. Now what do *you* wanta be? The school-teacher again . . . getting kissed by Marty?

DORIS (as RALPH puckers up his lips, shaking her head). We already did that scene.

RALPH (startled by Doris' show of strength). Hey . . . what's with little Doris?

DORIS. That's not my name anymore.

RALPH. But you're still my girl . . . right?

DORIS (coming to a decision). No. But I'm your good friend.

RALPH. *Friend*?

MONTGOMERY. Friends help.

DORIS (truly concerned). As a friend, I'd like to know what's happening to you.

RALPH (a burst of arrogance). Success! Success! (He starts off.) Hang on or hang up.

MONTGOMERY (after RALPH). Ralph! It's a bad scene. (Emphatically.) You are not Freddie.

RALPH (stopping). Listen! I'm . . . (He can't go on. The anger is going out of him. He doesn't want to go it alone.) You're right. Both of you. (Ruefully.) You know something? Even Freddie didn't want to be Freddie. (With a small smile.) He wanted to be Joe Namath. (He considers DORIS and MONTGOMERY.) And you were right about something else . . . (He holds open his arms.) . . . Friends do help! (He embraces DORIS and MONTGOMERY. Embarrassed, he breaks away.) Hey . . . I'll pick up a big pizza.

(MR. SHOROFSKY comes on R with BRUNO.)

DORIS (to MONTGOMERY, in shock). What was it I just did?

MONTGOMERY. I think maybe you just grew up.

DORIS (taking a deep breath, then starting off L). I think maybe I'll need that pizza.

MR. SHOROFSKY. If you plan to arrange this music for the senior class show, it can't be all in your head.

BRUNO (cheerfully). I agree. I told you. Music is not a solitary, isolated, private pleasure. Okay? You're right.

MR. SHOROFSKY (handing over the sheet music). Maybe these years with you haven't been entirely wasted. (As he goes, MONTGOMERY approaches BRUNO.)

MONTGOMERY (indicating the music). That's your arrangement? (BRUNO nods.) I've been working on the lyrics.

BRUNO. We'll have a few surprises . . .

MONTGOMERY. At the end, we'll ask the audience to join in the song. Every voice we can get . . .

(LEROY comes in.)

BRUNO. With Leroy leading the dance . . . (He is concerned as he sees LEROY.) Leroy?

LEROY (uptight). You seen Sherwood?

MONTGOMERY. What's the matter?

LEROY. I get a season with the Alvin Ailey Company . . . on graduation.

BRUNO. Great!

MONTGOMERY (getting the problem). You need Sherwood?

LEROY. I need graduation.

MONTGOMERY. She's with her husband. University Hospital . . . I think it's serious.

LEROY (starting off). I don't care.

MONTGOMERY (after LEROY). Leroy . . . (Too late. LEROY has gone off R. MONTGOMERY and BRUNO anxiously watch him go, then they, too, exit.)

(MRS. SHERWOOD comes on DL. She is tired and concerned. She pulls a chair down front and sits in it. She is very worried, so much so that she doesn't look up as LEROY enters. He crosses the stage and comes up to where she sits staring front. LEROY stands just to the side, hesitating to speak. She glances at him without recognition.)

MRS. SHERWOOD (after a moment, speaking tentatively). Leroy? Is it Leroy?

LEROY. You ever heard of Alvin Ailey?

MRS. SHERWOOD (uncertainly). He's a choreographer. What is it?

LEROY. He wants me to join his company.

MRS. SHERWOOD (flatly). Congratulations.

LEROY. I can't if you flunk me out.

MRS. SHERWOOD. Look, I'm sorry. I really don't think this is the time to . . .

LEROY. I *have* to graduate!

MRS. SHERWOOD. You should have thought of that four years ago.

LEROY. Where I come from, it don't pay to read and speak your way.

MRS. SHERWOOD. I can't deal with this. Not now, Leroy.

LEROY. Maybe I didn't say it right, but you've been down real hard on me.

MRS. SHERWOOD. Whatever you say, Leroy. Go home.

LEROY. I stopped going home a long time ago. But you didn't know that, did you?

MRS. SHERWOOD. Don't lecture, Leroy. Leave me alone. Let me sit here in peace and wait for my husband to die.

LEROY. You're going to hear it. I'm going to be a dancer . . . a good dancer.

MRS. SHERWOOD. Get out of here!

LEROY. You know who says so? Me. And you with your bitterness and your hangups aren't gonna —

MRS. SHERWOOD (pleading). Leave me alone!

LEROY. . . . keep me down 'cause I can't read stories I can see on t.v. every night of the week.

MRS. SHERWOOD (a cry). For God's sake! (She weeps, covering her face with her hands. LEROY watches for a moment. In spite of his anger, he feels her pain. He pulls up a chair and sits beside her as she tries to stifle her tears.)

LEROY (quietly). How's your old man?

MRS. SHERWOOD (fumbling for it). I can't find a handkerchief.

LEROY (handing his handkerchief to MRS. SHERWOOD).
Here . . . Here's mine. (MRS. SHERWOOD looks at it and
then starts mopping her eyes.)
MRS. SHERWOOD. Thank you.
LEROY (with a small smile). I got lotsa handkerchiefs. (MRS.
SHERWOOD looks at him. He reaches over and takes her hand
and holds it. She's grateful for the comfort. BOTH look
forward. After a moment, there's an emotion in LEROY that's
welling up out of him. Still looking forward, he begins to
speak with quiet, passionate conviction.) *You* are the only one
who ever cared a damn about anything I did. You always
wanted me to be better. You were too hard, but you only
wanted me to be better. (He takes a breath.) You are the only
one who ever cared . . . (As he and MRS. SHERWOOD continue to hold hands, both looking front, the light dims out on
them. In the dark, we hear the music of *America the Beautiful*.
This can come from a piano, a synthesizer, or from that and a
whole orchestra.)

(A spot of light comes up DC. MONTGOMERY walks into it.)

MONTGOMERY (to the audience). Now we come to the final
number in our senior class show . . . arranged and conducted
by Bruno Martelli who'll be going on to Juilliard. Choreography
by Leroy Johnson who just got a dazzling B minus on his last
essay. From here, he joins the Alvin Ailey Company.

(Lights come up to reveal the entire CAST, dressed for graduation. The STUDENTS are C, along with any available
EXTRAS. The FACULTY, PARENTS and RELATIVES are
at the side. BRUNO conducts from a podium, from his
synthesizer, or at a piano. The actual music can be recorded or

done by BRUNO or, if available, by a student orchestra. If an orchestra is used, it may include extra student musicians.)

MONTGOMERY.   *America the Beautiful* was written by Katharine Lee Bates when she was Professor of English at Wellesley College . . . to the old hymn tune *Materia*. It has been especially adapted for you by members of the graduating class at Performing Arts. (With this, BRUNO brings down his baton.   All available voices, along with the support of the music, join in a soaring presentation of this song. As it's sung, LEROY, HILARY, LYDIA and other DANCERS may dance to what is sung.)

ALL (first chorus traditionally).
O BEAUTIFUL FOR SPACIOUS SKIES
FOR AMBER WAVES OF GRAIN,
FOR PURPLE MOUNTAIN MAJESTIES
ABOVE THE FRUITED PLAIN!
AMERICA! AMERICA!
GOD SHED HIS GRACE ON THEE
AND CROWN THY GOOD
WITH BROTHERHOOD
FROM SEA TO SHINING SEA!

(Subsequent choruses move into a soft rock beat.)

CHORUS TWO: ALL.
AND BEAUTIFUL FOR MORE THAN THAT
FOR GIVING KIDS A CHANCE
TO WORK AND LEARN, FULFILL THEIR DREAMS
TO ACT OR SING OR DANCE.
AMERICA! AMERICA!

WE HEAR YOUR CASTING CALL
ALL RACES, CREEDS
TO FILL YOUR NEEDS,
YOU'VE GOT A PLACE FOR ALL.

CHORUS THREE:

MONTGOMERY. FROM ROMEO

BRUNO. TO ROCK AND ROLL

HILARY. FROM LES SYLPHIDES

LEROY. TO JAZZ

RALPH.
  THERE'S ROOM FOR EACH PERFORMER AND
  THE TALENT

BOYS. HE

GIRLS. SHE

ALL. HAS.
  AMERICA . . . PERFORMING ARTS

COCO. THEY'RE SIMILAR IT'S CLEAR

MONTGOMERY.
  NOT WHO YOU ARE
  BUT WHAT YOU DO

ALL. IS ALL THAT MATTERS HERE!

CHORUS FOUR:

SHOROFSKY.
  OUR BRUNO LEARNED RESPECT FOR BRAHMS

SHERWOOD. LEROY LEARNED HOW TO SPEAK

FARRELL. AND DORIS TO ASSERT HERSELF

DORIS. EXCUSE ME, DOMINIQUE!

TEACHERS. IT'S PLAIN TO SEE THE FACULTY

STUDENTS. ALTHOUGH THEY MAY SEEM STERN

TEACHERS. HAVE OPEN EARS TO YOUNG IDEAS

STUDENTS. AND EVEN TEACHERS LEARN.

CHORUS FIVE:

ALL.
  AND BEST OF ALL, THE FRIENDS WE MADE
  WE'LL KEEP THROUGH ALL OUR YEARS
  AND SIDE BY SIDE, WE'LL SHARE WITH THEM
  OUR LIVES AND OUR CAREERS.

(The music returns to the traditional beat; full, exciting sound.)

  AMERICA! AMERICA!
  GOD SHED HIS GRACE ON THEE
  AND CROWN THY GOOD
  WITH BROTHERHOOD
  FROM SEA TO SHINING SEA.

(As this last line is sung, MONTGOMERY and OTHERS may
  come down to the footlights, exhorting the audience to join in
  a repeat of the final stanza.)

MONTGOMERY. Please sing with us.

LEROY. Together.

DORIS. You know the words.

RALPH. One more time. (BRUNO now includes the audience
  with his baton. With all voices, including those in the audience

who join, and with all possible musical support, the final words
are sung — together!

AMERICA! AMERICA!
GOD SHED HIS GRACE ON THEE
AND CROWN THY GOOD
WITH BROTHERHOOD
FROM SEA TO SHINING SEA.

THE END

CREDITS

AMERICA THE BEAUTIFUL

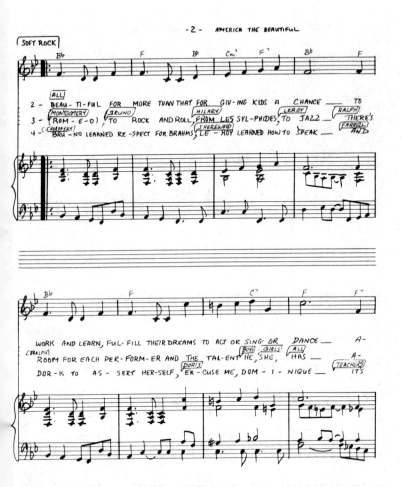

SOFT ROCK

2 - BEAU-TI-FUL FOR MORE THAN THAT FOR GIV-ING KIDS A CHANCE ___ TO
3 - (ROM-E-O), TO ROCK AND ROLL, FROM LES SYL-PHIDES, TO JAZZ ___ THERE'S
4 - BRU-NO LEARNED RE-SPECT FOR BRAHMS, LE-ROY LEARNED HOW TO SPEAK ___ AND

WORK AND LEARN, FUL-FILL THEIR DREAMS TO ACT OR SING OR DANCE ___ A-
ROOM FOR EACH PER-FORM-ER AND THE TAL-ENT HE, SHE, HAS ___ A-
DOR-IS TO AS-SERT HER-SELF, EX-CUSE ME, DOM-I-NIQUE ___ IT'S

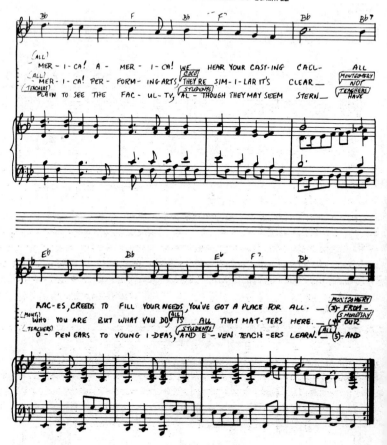

5- BEST OF ALL THE FRIENDS WE MADE WE'LL KEEP THRU ALL OUR YEARS __ AND

SIDE BY SIDE WE'LL SHARE WITH THEM OUR LIVES AND OUR CA - REERS __ A-

-MER-I-CA! A - MER-I-CA! GOD SHED HIS GRACE ON THEE__ AND

CROWN THY GOOD WITH BROTH-ER-HOOD, FROM SEA TO SHIN-ING SEA. __

DIRECTOR'S NOTES

DIRECTOR'S NOTES

DIRECTOR'S NOTES

DIRECTOR'S NOTES